Praise for *Trauma: The Invisible Epidemic*

"*Trauma: The Invisible Epidemic* will be a game changer. It provides not only the wisdom and intelligence of the author—an experienced professional in the worlds of psychiatry and sociology—but unlike other intellectual books written about trauma, Paul's offers a multitude of solutions. These practical responses to trauma address everything from physical and mental health to encouraging self-care and correcting unhealthy behaviors. Trauma affects countless individuals and families, and Paul's book is carefully thought out and explained in ways that are understandable to everyone. Wisdom and patience prevail in his unique outlook on a subject that has been largely ignored by doctors for years. It's a must-read for professionals as well as anyone who has experienced trauma or other psychological stressors."

TOMMY HILFIGER Entrepreneur, author, and philanthropist

"Dr. Conti is a physician and psychiatrist, and a person who has been through a lot, too. This gives him a unique perspective on how people function and how traumas can change us, specifically how traumas lead us to think and act differently without understanding why. Dr. Conti explains how trauma interacts with the way our brains work and how trauma is affected by certain aspects of society, and he does so with vivid illustrations of real people and their lives. But this book doesn't just stop there. Dr. Conti also provides real solutions—solutions people can use for themselves and their loved ones, and solutions to help make the world a kinder and safer place."

KIM KARDASHIAN Actress, producer, and businesswoman

"Paul Conti is one of the most unique and thoughtful physicians I have ever met. His approach to psychiatry is interactive both with the patient and with the referring physician. I have a large, successful concierge practice in New York and am often asked to see patients with complicated medical issues. Of all of the consultants I refer patients to, Paul is the most effective. Any time I have a patient with a complicated medical history and many previous evaluations, I reach out to Paul, who has taught me to look for and find the underlying trauma in their lives. Paul, my patients and I thank you for teaching me to be a better physician."

BERNARD KRUGER, MD Oncologist and cofounder of Sollis Health

"After reading Paul Conti's excellent book, *Trauma: The Invisible Epidemic*, I now understand that trauma exists in all of us. Sometimes we remember it, but even when we can't, it remembers us, keeping us from living our lives fully. Until we can identify it and bring it to the light, we exist with fears, anxieties, and masks that keep us from living in the light. Paul Conti's book helps us identify the trauma(s) we have endured in our lives and helps us move toward healing—no small task in today's traumatic world."

CAROLE BAYER SAGER Golden Globe- and Academy
Award-winning lyricist, singer, and songwriter

"I've known Paul Conti for nearly 25 years, and over the course of that time I have been privileged to witness, and benefit from, both his brilliance and his insight into the human condition. Paul has lived through terrible tragedies and, as such, can speak to the important subject of trauma as both a clinical expert and a regular person who has suffered and struggled as so many of us have. Paul's impact on my own life, and the lives of many of my patients, has been greater than I could ever explain on the back of a book jacket."

PETER ATTIA, MD Physician, consultant, and cofounder of Zero

trauma
the invisible epidemic

Paul Conti, MD

trauma
the invisible epidemic

**How Trauma Works and
How We Can Heal from It**

sounds true
BOULDER, COLORADO

Sounds True
Boulder, CO 80306

© 2021 Paul Conti

Foreword © 2021 Stefani Germanotta

Published 2021

Cover design by Jennifer Miles
Book design by Karen Polaski

Printed in the United States of America

Library of Congress Cataloging-in-Publication Data
Names: Conti, Paul (M.D.) author.
Title: Trauma: the invisible epidemic : how trauma works and
    how we can heal from it / Paul Conti, M.D.
Description: Boulder, CO : Sounds True, 2021. | Includes bibliographical references.
Identifiers: LCCN 2020057538 (print) | LCCN 2020057539 (ebook) | ISBN
    9781683647355 (trade paperback) | ISBN 9781683647362 (ebook)
Subjects: LCSH: Psychic trauma. | Psychic trauma—Treatment.
Classification: LCC RC552.T7 C664 2021 (print) | LCC
    RC552.T7 (ebook) | DDC 616.85/21—dc23
LC record available at https://lccn.loc.gov/2020057538
LC ebook record available at https://lccn.loc.gov/2020057539

10 9 8 7 6 5 4 3 2 1

To my daughters, Colette and Amelie

Those are the same stars, and that is the same moon,
that look down upon your brothers and sisters, and
which they see as they look up to them, though they
are ever so far away from us, and each other.

FROM *THE NARRATIVE OF SOJOURNER TRUTH*

Contents

Foreword

by Lady Gaga, Stefani Germanotta

I was gently thrown into an emergency care room at some private hospital in New York during a world tour. I remember a vision of a doctor and a nurse. They asked me calmly to count back from 100 as I continued to scream. I recall saying, "Why is no one panicking?" They encouraged me to keep counting back from 100 until I got to about 69. . . . I think. That's when I stopped counting and declared, "Hi, I'm Stefani." I also confessed that I couldn't feel my body, that I was completely numb.

I watched as their eyes gazed at a heart monitor, which I then realized I was connected to. They both did their best to hide their concern for the high level of my heart rate. I understood their concern, but I didn't have the wherewithal at the moment to be panicked about even one single thing more. I was in a deep state of disassociation from reality, and I was later told that I had a psychotic break.

"A doctor is coming," they assured me.

As I pleaded for medication (not knowing which one I wanted), I thought that certainly something strong could be made available to me. I felt incensed that they would not give any medicine to me until this "doctor" arrived.

Soon thereafter, someone entered the room. I noticed instantly it was a man, and also that he was not wearing a white coat and that there was no stethoscope in sight.

"Hello, I'm Dr. Paul Conti," he said. "I'm a psychiatrist."

I looked at the nurse who had been waiting with me, not realizing the other doctor had left the room a while ago.

"Why didn't you bring me a real doctor?" I asked the nurse.

Paul replied by saying, "I'm an Italian from New Jersey," and that was when I decided I was willing to talk to him. My dad is an Italian from New Jersey, so I figured I at least knew what I was dealing with.

At that moment, I began a journey that I have continued ever since, a journey with a man I had never met before but who would somehow make it part of his life's work to understand and help me. It wasn't until two years of working together that he revealed to me that he took six months to assess me and figure out if I was "moveable" when I was clearly in a state of traumatic paralysis.

I will not tell you everything that has happened between the two of us. But I will tell you this: Paul only wore his white coat when he needed to. To remind me he is a doctor. Most of the time, by mutual consent, Paul has related to me as a fellow human being and a safe man. We have learned about each other as we began a process of healing for me that I thought was impossible. I can now say with certainty that this man saved my life. He made life worth living. But most importantly, he empowered me to find and reclaim myself again. Whether Paul taught me this or we came up with it together, what I do know for sure is that women don't need men to simply give us help—we need men (and people who are not men as well) to believe in us in order for our traumas to heal.

Dr. Paul Conti is one of these men. He believes in women's stories, and the traumas they carry. He understands, as well, that trauma is not limited to any one demographic, that it is a human problem. And he believes in healing. Paul is kind, and we could all learn from his kindness. Once I began to see this in him, I knew healing was possible. I'm on that journey now, and so are you.

Introduction

Like you, I've experienced quite a bit since I first came into this world (for me, fifty or so years ago on the second floor of St. Francis Hospital in Trenton, New Jersey). Much of it has been joyful, but a lot has been difficult and emotionally painful. I see myself as a regular person who has been through some tragic experiences, felt them deeply, and thought about them a great deal. I am a physician and practicing psychiatrist with training in brain biology and psychology, and I approach my profession from a holistic point of view. I've had the privilege of being alongside countless people going through intense and often life-changing situations. All of these relationships are personal to me, and through these relationships and my own experience, I've come to think the way I do about trauma and the devastating role it plays in our lives.

Before deciding to apply to medical school, I had a career in business. My only experience with health care to that point involved visiting older relatives in the hospital—mostly first- and second-generation Italian immigrants, some who served our country in World War II (you'll hear all about my Uncle Rango in chapter 5). As they aged, these relatives needed more care than they were used to receiving from trusted local doctors, and the shift to visiting hospitals wasn't easy on any of us. The doctors and nurses always seemed so busy and remote, and they rarely communicated with us.

When they did, we often struggled to decipher what they meant, and I was often left feeling intimidated and confused. I knew there had to be kinder, better ways to treat people in such difficult situations, but at the time I'd never have guessed that I'd eventually devote so much of my life to paying attention to people and doing my best to help.

My father is a businessman, so it seemed practical that I'd become one, too. I eventually got a job at a first-rate consulting firm, but after a while in the field I began to feel stagnant and trapped. It felt like all of my options were played out, and everything was going to be downhill from there on out. I became depressed. I was only twenty-five. And that's when my youngest brother killed himself.

Jonathan was twenty. He shot himself in the home we grew up in with a handgun my father had been issued during the Korean War. My mother found his body.

After the shock decreased, my family and I tried to understand what seemed like such a senseless tragedy. My brother and his girlfriend had recently broken up, and we believed he might have been experimenting with drugs, but these issues didn't explain Jonathan's decision to take his own life. In retrospect, I understand much better.

Four years earlier, a rare congenital problem had shut down Jonathan's entire digestive tract. Up until that point, he had been perfectly healthy. Now here he was—sixteen years old, his life in danger, and having to go in and out of Children's Hospital of Philadelphia for one painful procedure after another. He couldn't eat. He lost an unbelievable amount of weight and strength. He was scared. The entire ordeal was horribly traumatic for him. Later on, people who knew Jonathan before his illness would comment on how much he'd changed.

I hadn't seen Jonathan much when I was away at college, but even in the years before his suicide, I was clueless as to what was going on with him. Jonathan wanted me to see him as strong and happy, so he hid his trauma from me (or, more accurately, he hid what he understood of his trauma). I'm not sure I would've noticed much anyway. Like I said, I was depressed at the time. I was lost in my own self-soothing strategies and largely blind to my own tribulations and trauma.

After Jonathan's death, I gradually learned about the history of mental illness and suicide in my family. I spent a lot more time with my parents and my other (now only) brother, and I started to realize some things about how

I'd been living my life up to that point. I began to see how I'd existed under a litany of *shoulds* born of fear—fear that I wouldn't succeed, fear that I would lament leaving a good job, fear that I wouldn't know what I was doing and would regret it later. After my brother's death, those fear-based shoulds governing my life faded away, and I couldn't remember why they had been so important in the first place. And that's when I decided to explore my long-held fascination with becoming a physician.

Although it was at times arduous, medical school was a wonderful experience. I was eager to learn all the things I didn't know when my elder relatives were getting sick—all the things I didn't know when my brother was sick. And I wanted to wield this secret knowledge so that I could finally make a difference, one person at a time. As I rotated through different specialties during the last two years of medical school, I was struck over and over again by how the world inside of a person determines so much of their outside world. I began to see how our life choices and experiences of life emerge from whatever is going on inside of us, and I became amazed by the number of problems—some of them fatal—that were entirely preventable. Medical school taught me about the astonishing complexity of human beings, from head to toe, as well as the predictability of many of the preventable things that hurt or kill us—a poor diet, for example, or chronic smoking, or car accidents.

The more I learned about clinical medicine and spent time with patients, the more appalled I became by how mental health factors regularly went unaddressed, leading to both mental and physical pain and sometimes death. I saw how people were suffering and dying not just from physical illness but from underlying mental health factors that contributed to their issues in the first place. So often it was clear that there were better ways to approach medical problems—any problems, for that matter—by paying attention to the underlying issues. More often than not, this meant paying attention to trauma.

I became interested in psychiatry because it excited me to think about combining brain biology, medicine, and psychology to understand and help people. Psychiatrists need to think about medical and neurological conditions that sometimes are the root cause of what leads people to seek care or be brought to care, and they also have to focus on how the mind and body influence each other constantly. For example, the physical suffering my brother had to deal with affected his mind, and those changes resulted in behaviors that affected both his body and mind even more. I decided to become a psychiatrist because I wanted to make a difference for people like my brother.

WHY I WROTE THIS BOOK AND WHAT I HOPE YOU GET FROM IT

The diversity of human problems I have witnessed in my life and career is nearly infinite. That being said, one reason stands out for the vast majority of these problems—the underlying reason is trauma.

That's a bold statement, and it's meant to be. The message I'm here to deliver about trauma should be bold because it's meant to change your life, and the lives of others, for the better. I believe it's also a relieving statement. Think about what it would be like if all the lights went off in your neighborhood—what a pain it would be if the solution required you to go around replacing every last light in every single house! Repairing the transformer might seem like a heavy lift, but it's a much more reasonable solution to the problem you'd be facing. That's how it is with trauma, too.

I wrote this book to sound the alarm about trauma. Trauma is way too prevalent, harmful, contagious, and often invisible—just like a virus. And if we keep ignoring that fact and allowing trauma to remain hidden, I wouldn't bet on our ever defeating it.

Sure, most of us already know about trauma. This certainly isn't the first book about it, and we regularly hear or read about trauma in the news. However, I think most of the ways we encounter the conversation around trauma resemble screaming through a megaphone—megaphones get our attention, but they're overly alarming and annoying, and they usually just leave us shocked or confused. That's not what I want to do here. This book is designed to really talk about trauma, to foster actual dialogue after you put away the computer or newspaper for the day. I'm putting down the megaphone so we can have a thoughtful conversation.

Okay, technically this isn't a conversation—I wrote this book, and now you're reading it, so it isn't exactly a two-way exchange of ideas. Still, I want it to feel like a dialogue, and I offer the practices and reflections in these chapters with that in mind. It's my belief that we currently aren't given adequate strategies to deal with trauma; neither are we provided the understanding and motivation we need to create necessary change in ourselves, others, and the world. With that in mind, here's what I want you to get out of this book:

- A thorough understanding of trauma and shame
- The ability to recognize trauma in yourself, others, and the society around you
- Knowledge of the ways in which individual and collective trauma operate on a societal level
- Motivation to stop trauma in its tracks
- Lots of practical tools to help yourself and others

In addition to being packed with stories from my life and the lives of my patients, this book is full of descriptions and explications broken down into four distinct parts. Part I: What Trauma Is and How It Works defines trauma, explores different types of trauma, and lays out the crucial role shame plays in it. Part II: The Big Picture—The Sociology of Trauma zooms out to show you how big and pervasive the problem of trauma actually is. I discuss how the current state of health care is ill-equipped to handle trauma; I also explore how social conditions such as the Covid-19 pandemic and racism foster even more trauma. In Part III: An Owner's Manual for Your Brain, I get into the role of the limbic system, specifically how trauma alters our brain biology, emotions, memories, and physical experience of illness and pain. Finally, Part IV: How We Can Beat Trauma—Together is a call to action to process, purge, and heal trauma's detrimental effects for all of us.

PART ONE

WHAT TRAUMA IS AND HOW IT WORKS

———

Human suffering anywhere concerns
men and women everywhere.

ELIE WIESEL, *NIGHT*

CHAPTER 1

How We Talk About Trauma

---

trauma \trau-muh\ *noun* anything that causes emotional or physical pain and leaves its mark on a person as life moves forward.

Trauma affects everything. An alarming percentage of us has been significantly hurt in ways that cannot be seen from the outside. I don't mean trivial hurt, like someone giving you the wrong flavor of ice cream or eating your last cookie. By trauma, I'm referring to the type of emotional or physical pain that often goes unseen, yet actually changes our brain biology and psychology. And although humans tend to be pretty resilient, many of us suffer from these traumatic changes in more ways and for longer than we imagine.

ANALOGIES FOR TRAUMA

Sometimes a working definition alone doesn't cut it, so I often use analogies to talk about trauma, illustrate how it works, and help lay out a path toward what to do about it. Here are some of my favorite analogies, but you'll find several more scattered throughout the book.

The Trauma Virus

I probably use this analogy the most, and it's certainly germane at the time I'm writing this book. I've been thinking of trauma as an epidemic for years now, but recently the Covid-19 pandemic has hit home everywhere, and I've started considering trauma as being like a virus that also leaves far too many people dead and suffering aftereffects in its wake. As with Covid, you can't see trauma itself; you just see it at work—silently but maliciously. As it harms one person, it replicates and jumps to another; then it spreads to another and often back again. Unfortunately, there aren't vaccine trials for trauma, and early testing for trauma is woefully lacking. And until we employ all of the tools at our disposal and finally face the threat of the trauma virus, not only will our happiness and well-being remain threatened but also our survival.

Covid has profoundly changed the way we experience the world and relate to our other community members: We wear masks when we're with others, we maintain physical distance from them (usually six feet or more), we wonder if they might be infectious agents, we keep conversations short, and so on. Trauma's impacts aren't all that different: Because we suffer from anxiety and depression as a result of trauma, we wear metaphorical masks to deal with people (in Rome, theatrical masks were called *personas*), we maintain emotional distance from them, we sometimes avoid people who appear to be suffering from anxiety or depression of their own, and we keep conversations with them brief and shallow.

A wise response to a viral pandemic is to become more closed until a vaccine becomes widely available.
A wise response to a trauma pandemic is to become more open so that we ourselves become the vaccine.

Before Covid hit, I always thought of pandemics as times when people set aside differences to come together to fight a common enemy. In the past, I imagined, people must have listened to their doctors and nurses and followed guidelines set by community authorities to take care of their loved ones and others. I'm writing this in 2020, and it has been a rude awakening.

Too many people don't appear inspired by any notion of the common good. In fact, the news is full of folks who seem to have doubled down on whatever preferences and grudges they hold, all the while ignoring the lethal threat growing day by day. Our national response to the Covid virus has been marked by denial, squabbling, and a shocking refusal to face unpleasant truths. Our government didn't look ahead, even when warned. And because we weren't willing to face inconvenient truths, we eliminated countless opportunities to stave off avoidable tragedies. By any legitimate standard, we failed as a nation to get out of our own way and to do what was right for our country and everyone in it.

I'm deeply troubled by this. But it also makes me all the more determined to get the message out about the trauma virus, which is also a pandemic generating untold misery and desperation around the world.

Trauma might not be getting the press Covid is at the moment, and that makes it all the more deadly. Like Covid, the trauma virus itself is invisible. We might be able to recognize some of its symptoms, but because trauma actually alters our brains—our thoughts and memories and their meanings—it's even more difficult to recognize the extent of its damage. Most of us think of trauma as something that results from a significant, one-time event, but that's just the tip of the trauma iceberg. The scientists who study trauma tell us there's a lot more to it than the obvious stuff we can see, but—as the Covid pandemic has shown—we're not always the best at listening to scientists.

One thing scientists tell us about the trauma virus is that it is harmful enough to affect the children of the future—children who aren't even imagined yet, let alone born. Trauma can define how genetic characteristics are passed on, meaning that the consequences of trauma are being written into our future genetic record today. So trauma acts like a pandemic that extends beyond a person's death. We're looking at a virus that infiltrates the survival chain of our very species, allowing its harm to amplify across generations.

Masks and isolation serve us well in a viral pandemic. They protect us by limiting the spread of illness so that we can survive and move life forward. The masks and isolation imposed by trauma, however, mostly operate on the inside, replacing healthy emotions and thoughts with negative ones and projecting our discomfort and fears upon the world. None of this serves us well or protects us. Instead, the masks and isolation associated with trauma foster even more trauma, allowing the seeds of our suffering to grow and spread. This is how the trauma pandemic perpetuates itself.

A wise response to a viral pandemic is to become more closed until a vaccine becomes widely available. A wise response to a trauma pandemic is to become more open so that we ourselves become the vaccine. Opening ourselves to understanding, to compassion, and to change lets in the psychological sunlight and fresh air we need to thrive.

Although the virus analogy most accurately captures the danger and severity of trauma, I sometimes like to use two other comparisons to describe just how serious a threat trauma is to all of us.

Pollution

Trauma is a lot like the air we breathe—it's everywhere, flowing in and out of our homes and our bodies and the bodies of our loved ones. We usually don't think very much about the air we breathe unless the pollution levels rise (smog in our cities, for example, or smoke from forest fires in our neighborhoods), and it gets unhealthy to take into our bodies. That's why we use the air quality index (AQI) to track major pollutants such as ground-level ozone, carbon monoxide, aerosols, and so on. That being said, most of the time we pay virtually no attention to the air we need to survive. That's similar to our approach to trauma, too—we only recognize it as serious when symptoms get out of hand. What would be ideal is some form of ongoing monitoring system that empowers us to understand trauma's day-to-day effects and helps us to minimize the damage trauma causes in our internal and external environments.

Of course, pollution is also a major problem in water. Imagine placing a drop of colored dye in a large bowl of water. In this case, the dye is toxic, and if you watch the bowl closely, you can see the toxin disperse throughout the water. When the dye first drops into the water, the color is rich and bright, but its intensity decreases as the toxin spreads throughout the bowl. There's still the same amount of poison in the water, and it still goes with the water wherever it travels, but it might seem like less of a big deal than it did at first—after all, the color of the dye isn't nearly as obvious as it once was.

Just because we aren't immediately aware of or concerned about pollution doesn't mean that it isn't a danger to our planet. And just because we aren't paying attention to trauma doesn't meant that it isn't working to undermine our well-being. The threat is real, and trauma is actively doing damage at this very moment.

Parasites

Sometimes the trauma parasite is so bad that we even forget the basics of how to keep ourselves safe.

The third analogy I want to talk about is *toxoplasma*. Toxoplasma is a parasite that goes through different stages of development in different hosts. This allows it to live and reproduce by using the hosts it invades, ensuring its future survival. We can identify the stages of development of the parasite—its life cycle—as well as how the host at any one stage is used to deliver the parasite forward to the next stage. Toxoplasma is fascinating because its life cycle doesn't merely involve different hosts—the parasite uses different species to propel its spread.

Toxoplasma has evolved to transfer from mice to cats (and sometimes even from cats to humans). The parasite didn't consciously plan it, of course, but nonetheless it developed a way to increase the chances that mice get eaten by cats, and it did so by changing the brains of infected mice to be less afraid of cats. It's hard not to marvel at how ingeniously devious this is—after all, mice have an instinctual fear of cats. Yet a mouse infected with toxoplasma loses this fear without knowing it, such that it might simply saunter by a cat without a care in the world.

I believe trauma does to humans what toxoplasma does to mice. It might not get us eaten by cats, but trauma certainly changes our brains to make us forget some fundamental aspects about what it means to be fully alive—it makes us forget our worth, our dreams, our gifts, and our aspirations. And sometimes the trauma parasite is so bad that we even forget the basics of how to keep ourselves safe. I can't count how many times I've seen a person physically hurt in a previous relationship (and terrified of being abused like that again) enter a new relationship in which being physically abused is nearly certain.

Trauma alters our brains in ways not unlike those by which toxoplasma makes mice less aware of the obvious danger of cats. Instead of paying attention to the warning signs in others, traumatized people often get focused on changing themselves—on acting and being "better" (with little help from society in this regard, too). This thinking just generates more shame, self-blame, and fantasies that a new relationship can be made healthy and safe, which often lead an abused person to discount or ignore warning signs that might as well be on a neon billboard. The signs clearly indicate that more abuse, despair, and shame are ahead, but trauma causes people to mistakenly think that changing themselves will change how other people behave toward them.

Like toxoplasma, trauma does what it does in order to survive. It might not be capable of conscious thought, but that doesn't make it any less dangerous or effective. Toxoplasma has evolved to create more toxoplasma no matter what. In the same way, trauma makes more trauma, moving from human to human, from humans to other living beings and the planet, and back to humans again. And it will keep doing so until we stop it.

PRE-EXISTING CONDITIONS

Just as viruses, pollution, and parasites affect each of us differently, so does trauma. Trauma comes in various forms, frequencies, and intensities, and there are numerous reasons some of us are more affected than others. If we want to beat trauma, we'll need to explore these factors and understand them thoroughly. Most people are better prepared for one type of trauma than another—more able to use life experience to fight one type of enemy well—whereas they might be defenseless against another type of enemy.

Our genetics and life experiences factor into what's known as the *multiple-hit hypothesis*. This hypothesis, which can be applied to a number of real-life situations, states that our coping mechanisms are weakened by successive traumatic experiences—essentially, how many "hits" we've taken. Some people are profoundly affected by their first trauma experience, whereas others might appear remarkably resilient only to be affected by a seemingly less severe experience later. People who suffer from ethnic prejudice or systemic racism, for example, experience an unending barrage of stressors that ratchets up their vulnerability to more trauma. When it comes to taking hits, we're often not aware of how they accumulate for ourselves and others.

I'VE GOT A STORY TO TELL

As I mentioned in the Introduction, this book is full of stories from my life and the lives of people I've had the honor of knowing. Like the analogies just discussed, I use stories to illustrate how trauma operates as well as how people struggle with—and triumph over—trauma. These stories are powerful because they are real. I've altered some aspects to protect confidentiality, but I've remained true to the experiences as I have understood them (and in some cases lived them). We all have stories. We use them to remember and share the joyful events in our lives as well as our challenges. And stories of trauma and how people live with trauma are as old as the moon. Trauma is the villain we meet on our quest for happiness; trauma does the damage that changes us and reinforces the anxieties we carry. On the surface, this seems to negatively affect an internal scale that we work to tip back toward happiness, but that's just one part of the story.

Trauma hijacks our stories.

The part of the trauma story we too often ignore involves changes to our brain biology and psychology, and the reason we ignore these effects is because trauma itself prevents us from seeing these changes and how their consequences play out in our lives. Trauma eats away at our dreams and colors our decisions without us even knowing it. In this way, trauma is like a villain or enemy that sets up house inside of us. This enemy makes us feel conflicted about who we are, what we are capable of achieving, and what we deserve. It messes with our relationship to the scale itself—adding extra weight to the negative side of life, cheating us out of our birthright of safety and joy, and doing so all the while without us having any idea that this is happening. Trauma changes our emotions and memories, and changed emotions and memories alter our decisions and the courses of our lives.

When people under my care have died, I have often thought about the surface story of their death compared with what trauma was doing to them behind the scenes. This is nowhere more evident than in their listed cause of death. For example, the official version might be *car accident* as opposed to *raped by coworker*, or *suicide* instead of *swindled out of his life savings*, or *cirrhosis of the liver* in the place of *child abuse by an alcoholic parent*. Trauma hijacks our stories in life and also in death.

FOUR VIGNETTES

Here are four real-world stories about trauma (two from my own life) to illustrate trauma's effects.

- I had dissected a pancreas in medical school and knew its function, but the organ had no special meaning to me until my mother was diagnosed with pancreatic cancer. After an extremely difficult time for my family, my mother died. Up until her diagnosis, she had been healthy and active, reading voraciously and walking so fast I could not keep up with her. Now, whenever I hear the word *pancreas*, my muscles tense, my breathing gets faster, and I see images of her funeral and the place on my parents' couch where she isn't anymore. You can't tell from the outside, but I sure can tell from the inside. One time in London I found myself not wanting to meet a friend at the St. Pancras Railway Station because *Pancras* was a little too close to that dreaded word. I went anyway, but I began to feel guilty on the walk there, thinking "I should have gone home more often while Mom was sick." The truth was that I had gone home regularly (from the West Coast to the East Coast and back) every two weeks for many months. I went to medical appointments with her and on outings with Mom and Dad. I helped to take care of her as she became more ill. Regardless, I still felt guilty, and automatically so—like a reflex.

- I have taken care of more people who have been sexually assaulted than I could ever count, and the trauma they experience reaches into every facet of their lives. One patient of mine was leaving a friend's party and was raped in a dark corner of the front lawn as she was heading to her car. She particularly remembers that there were no trees on the lawn, no hiding places, and yet she had not seen the man who attacked her. It was dark and late, and most people had already left, but she stayed longer because it was fun talking to some new people with similar interests. They were talking about rock climbing. After the attack, she suffered from panic attacks, had trouble concentrating, and worried about getting fired from her job for poor performance. She dreaded the upcoming time change because that meant it would be dark outside whenever she was walking to her car to go to work or to return home. She felt threatened by virtually every man she met, even the ones who loved her and whom she loved. She had begun to dress down so as not to draw attention to herself, but as a result she was barely meeting the minimum dress standards of her company. Worst of all, she felt guilty. She knew it wasn't her fault, but she couldn't help ruminating about what she might have done differently—gone home earlier, been more careful as she left, dressed differently? But she felt most guilty about feeling afraid when her own brother wanted to give her a hug. And she certainly didn't want to date or go rock climbing.

- When I was in my twenties, I traveled a lot, which involved numerous airplane takeoffs and landings. Once, as I was getting ready to fly back home from Europe, I remember feeling congested, so I took some sort of decongestant. Unbeknownst to me, I was suffering from sinusitis, and that, in addition to the pressure changes created during takeoffs and landings, had further weakened my sinus lining. As the plane descended for a stopover in Amsterdam, my lining tore open, blood filled a sinus cavity, and it began pressing extremely hard on the nerves running to my left upper teeth. The pain was so terrible that I actually lost consciousness a few times, and I must have been quite the spectacle as we slowly crossed the Atlantic. To this day, I'm still afraid of takeoffs and landings, worrying that something will burst inside of me and that the pain will be unbearable. When I think about this story, I also recall the proper and reserved Dutch family seated next to me, and I wonder how my suffering affected the two girls (both about eight years old, each with a bow in her hair), who had to witness some random guy in such a state of misery for nine whole hours.

- One of my elderly patients was always accompanied to my office by her affable husband. She brought me cookies around the holidays, and her husband would assure me that there were no tastier cookies in existence. There were several parks in the area where they had been walking together for years. One day, without warning, her husband fell to the ground and did not move. My patient was terrified. She desperately tried to find a pulse, started CPR, and called 911 all at once, but he died right there from a massive heart attack. So much was taken from her, but what tormented her the most was that she couldn't go back to any of the parks they used to frequent. Her best memories were now weapons against her, and she felt guilty as well. Should she have noticed something different in him? Could she have done something different to save his life? Anything that reminded her of his death would guarantee a night of terrible insomnia and bad dreams that she couldn't remember. Years later, she's much better, but she still hasn't been to a park.

These examples of trauma are each quite different—one involves a purposeful attack on an innocent woman, one involves excruciating physical pain, and two are events that resulted in the death of a loved one (one slowly, the other suddenly).

Common threads run through these events as well. One is the high level of negative emotions, and another is a *changed world*—a post-trauma world that can feel and therefore look dramatically different after the event. Once pleasant thoughts became charged with negative emotions, as did previously neutral ideas. The woman in the second example couldn't even go rock climbing anymore because of the proximity of a conversation about rock climbing to the traumatic event itself. Airplane landings were previously neutral to me, but not after blood filled a sinus cavity during a landing and caused an awful amount of pain. The word pancreas is now infused with guilt and loss for me, and an elderly woman can't bear visiting parks without her deceased love.

These are just some of the ways trauma changes our experience of the outside world. Regardless of the nature or severity of the traumatic event, our before and after stories couldn't be more different.

CHAPTER 2

Types of Trauma and Post-Trauma Syndromes

Some people who contract a life-threatening virus will become ill very quickly, whereas others won't show symptoms until the damage has spread far and wide. With this in mind, it's important to understand that there are different types of trauma so we can recognize them and discern how they are similar to each other as well as how they are different.

ACUTE TRAUMA

Acute trauma results from a particular event that most people would recognize as severe: a vicious attack, an injury in combat, witnessing violent death, a bad car accident, a life-threatening medical crisis. In each of these, something occurs that creates a radically different experience of life than what came before it. Acute trauma is often accompanied by fear, pain, horror, intense vulnerability, and losing the illusion that we can predict or control life in such a way as to ward off disaster. People can be understandably distraught during and immediately following such an event, but sometimes people are eerily calm, as if a mental circuit breaker has been flipped or the brain has taken itself offline in order to avoid becoming overwhelmed. Whether or not a person gets professional help later on, they are usually quite aware that something impactful has happened to them, and their life is noticeably different than it was before.

CHRONIC TRAUMA

Instead of one big event, chronic trauma comes from prolonged exposure to harmful situations and people: living under siege in wartime, experiencing ongoing sexual abuse as a child, enduring prejudice and racism, and so on. It isn't uncommon for a person suffering from chronic trauma not to be aware of it or not to realize they've been living in traumatic circumstances until much later. Of course, sometimes we're quite aware of things our brains suppress, pushing them below the surface of consciousness, because we can't bear to live with the knowledge. It's like the trauma is an air-filled ball we keep trying to push beneath the surface of the water—it takes a lot of work to keep the ball down, and sometimes it bursts to the surface with enough force to hurt us. Among other things, chronic trauma can result in ongoing self-doubt, hopelessness, insecurity, fear, negativity about the world, and shame (we'll look at shame in a lot more detail in chapter 3). Both acute and chronic trauma pave the way for shame, but chronic trauma allows shame to hide better.

I think of all the people I've met in emergency rooms and clinics seeking refuge from abusive living situations. Many of them receive the care they need, seek help for their chronic trauma, and go on to live rewarding lives. Unfortunately, far too many of them return to their abusers or find themselves in other abusive relationships because chronic trauma can fool people into believing they don't have options or they don't deserve better. Sometimes even the thought of a better life can feel like a cruel mockery to be avoided at all costs—like when a starving person won't eat the food placed in front of them because it has been yanked away so often.

VICARIOUS TRAUMA

We have the wonderful capacity to feel the emotions of others and to help them heal by extending our love and compassion, but we can also be harmed when we internalize their suffering. Several tragedies from medical school come to mind—when I think about them, the memories are so strong that the boundary between what happened to me and what happened to other people becomes blurred. Vicarious trauma affects first responders and people in other helping professions, but it can also affect any compassionate person who doesn't shy away from the suffering of others. Being present with others can alleviate their pain and aloneness, but it can also let in their terror, and that terror can imprint in ways that mimic the direct experience of trauma. Of course, not everyone who is compassionate is personally affected by external suffering, or at least not equally. It depends on the types of trauma a given person has experienced themselves as well as how finely tuned their emotional compass is.

POST-TRAUMA SYNDROMES

When we think of trauma's long-term impacts, we often think of post-traumatic stress disorder (PTSD). PTSD is an acronym that gets used a lot in the media, and many people associate it with trauma even if they don't know exactly what it means. However, most people aren't aware that PTSD is just one of many ongoing issues that can result from trauma.

A more meaningful way to think about the long-term impact of trauma is to consider the idea of *post-trauma syndromes*. By post-trauma syndromes, I'm referring to the array of problems that affect a person's life in a negative way after trauma occurs, and PTSD is just one of these problems. Post-trauma syndromes can arise from acute, chronic, or vicarious trauma. Although treatable, many post-trauma syndromes are never identified by the people who suffer from them, their family and friends, or the professionals who treat them. And unless we can identify the problem, it typically gets worse.

Here are seven criteria that establish what constitutes a post-trauma syndrome. The first two describe the experience of trauma, whereas the subsequent five criteria describe symptoms we can recognize in ourselves and in others.

1 **EXPOSURE.** This criterion might seem straightforward, but this is not always the case. Acute trauma is often easy to identify, but chronic and vicarious trauma can prove difficult to pin down, especially when we add in the denial factor. We might be unable to admit to ourselves that we have been traumatized because the shame generated by the trauma can convince us that things will be worse if we acknowledge it. Shame also tells us that it was our fault, that people won't believe us, that we should remain quiet because other people have it worse, that

we should just focus on the positive things in life, and so on. Shame uses endless arguments to keep us stuck in the grip of our trauma.

2 **RE-EXPERIENCE.** Trauma re-experience means that a person continues to be haunted by what happened to them in the past. Some hauntings are more obvious than others. Sometimes we're quite clear on how our traumas are weaving their way through our minds, changing thoughts and feelings. This is most obvious after acute trauma. We know that we are different than before the trauma, and one of the worst things about that experience is confusion about who we are, feeling alienated from the self we're accustomed to knowing. We can feel lost and desperate to regain control, and the fear generated by our thoughts during the experience can lead to even greater fear and shame, fueling trauma re-experience and making it even harder to admit what's happening and get help. It's easier in the moment, and it often seems safer, to push the fear below the surface and move forward, hoping it will just go away. It's even more difficult if the situation is less obvious, which happens more frequently with chronic and vicarious trauma. It can take time for us to put together cause and effect, and we might not understand what's going on—why we're having the thoughts and feelings we're experiencing. Some of our decisions might even alarm us.

3 **HYPERVIGILANCE.** We all have a threat sensor that usually lies below the surface of awareness that constantly surveys the sights, sounds, and sensations of our internal and external environment. You can be engaged in a relaxing activity like reading a book or watching a movie, but if that threat sensor sees an unexpected shadow or hears something suspicious in the next room, it will let you know immediately. Its purpose is to protect us but not really bother the conscious part of our minds unless the threat calls for vigilance. When people suffer from trauma, however, their threat sensor becomes hyperactive and hypervigilant, convincing them that things are dangerous and wrong *right now*, constantly. It's like the threat sensor recognizes that it was unable to prevent the initial trauma, and now it's trying to make up for it by being active and loud all the time. But like the boy who cried wolf,

when the threat sensor is always sounding the alarm, the brain eventually becomes fatigued and unable to differentiate false from real danger. Hypervigilance also results in ongoing tension, less enjoyment and ease, an increase in risk taking, and physical issues such as high blood pressure, heart disease, stroke, and cancer.

4 **INCREASED BASELINE ANXIETY.** Whereas hypervigilance is specifically overactivation of the brain's threat-sensing function, trauma can raise baseline levels of anxiety as well. By anxiety, here I am referring to an internal feeling of tension and discomfort that can diminish our ability to counter distress by using healthy coping skills. Anxiety can also negatively affect our coping skills by diminishing our perseverance, our ability to maintain self-confidence in the face of challenges, and our ability to orient toward self-soothing when we get upset or frazzled. The higher our baseline anxiety, the less we're able to access these coping skills. It's not too different from being out of shape and suffering from stiff joints and muscular tension—if we need to jump out of danger's way, we're not going to do so very skillfully. Additionally, increases in our baseline anxiety also lower distress tolerance, which refers to the amount of distress a person can put up with and still use good coping skills and make healthy decisions. Distress can come from vivid memories of the trauma that play over and over again in our mind or from trauma-induced worries that we'll fail in our endeavors and feel embarrassed. External examples of distress can include partners whose behavior reminds us of past abusers, experiencing bullying or prejudice, or being subjected to sexual harassment at work. Regardless of the form our distress takes, we're better able to face it through a strategy of healthy thoughts, compassion, and smart decisions.

Trauma changes the whole internal playing field. Just as an athlete can't perform as well under adverse conditions (a muddy playing field or high winds, for example), we're not at our best when trauma undermines our ability to function by throwing too much at us and messing with the control panels of our nervous systems. The difference here is that an athlete will return to optimal performance when conditions return to normal, whereas trauma increases the likelihood of negative changes to body and mind.

5 **DECREASED BASELINE MOOD.** Mood and anxiety are strongly related. Trauma exposure, trauma re-experience, and hypervigilance all turn up the dial for anxiety while simultaneously turning down the dial for mood. When we suffer from trauma, we become more prone to avoidance and isolation, which leads to decreased enjoyment of previously pleasurable activities. It isn't hard to roll the tape forward and see where this is going. How many times have I heard a person describe themselves in words unimaginable before the traumatic event? One previously social person now described himself as someone who "lays low because people just don't like me." Another well-liked and formerly gregarious patient described herself as "never getting along with anyone, so it's not even worth trying." In each case the person looked surprised in the midst of uttering these phrases, and upon reflection they couldn't tell if the words were false or if they became true at some point after the trauma occurred. This is just one more way trauma fools us about ourselves, using anxiety and a low mood to camouflage its actions.

6 **INADEQUATE SLEEP.** Trauma attacks our sleep from every angle—it increases how long it takes to fall asleep and how many times we wake up during the night, and it decreases the length and quality of our sleep. This is obviously bad for our happiness and health—fatigue is correlated with an increase in injuries and accidents—and it often means more anxiety and dread while we're trying to get the sleep we so desperately need. In turn, this can lead to more foggy decision making, avoidance, and the self-fulfilling prophesies of loneliness and disappointment. Our mental and physical health can decline, each compounding the negative effects of the other. Poor sleep is also associated with rumination—those unproductive, negative, repetitive thoughts: It'll never work out, for example, or I'm a terrible person. The more we repeat these things to ourselves, the more likely we are to believe them and act from those erroneous beliefs, especially when we consider that rumination happens both consciously and unconsciously. A person can find themselves wide awake in the middle of the night, thinking the same negative thoughts repeatedly, becoming more distressed about being awake and miserable, and not even realizing that the rumination has been going on just under the surface of sleep for hours. Needless to say, this destroys the restorative function of sleep.

7 **BEHAVIOR CHANGE.** I've talked about changes in behavior in most of the criteria above, but I think it deserves its own category as well. This is because behavior changes quickly add up, multiply, and eventually lead us to unrecognized places with no obvious escape. In other words, trauma makes us changed people without our understanding the extent, risk, or damage. People often comment about how different they are after experiencing trauma, and they have trouble uncovering the good parts about the people they once were. The way we act in the world affects the way we think and feel about ourselves, and thoughts and feelings change our behavior in turn. It's like using a map that's just a little bit "off." Following a map like that might get us to our destination in a roundabout way, but more often than not, it gets us confused and lost.

People suffering from post-trauma syndromes might experience all seven of these criteria or sometimes just the first two plus some combination of the others. In all cases, there are real changes in the person that cause unhappiness, increase suffering and risk, and decrease ease and resilience. These negative changes strike at the foundation of our very existence. Individually and collectively, this is what we're up against. This is what we have to address if we truly want to triumph over trauma.

Sometimes There Is No Vacation

A long time ago, my wife and I planned a brief vacation—a long weekend away in a peaceful setting. We both really needed it. I felt desperate for a break from the constant responsibility of phones and pagers scaring me with emergencies during the day (and sometimes throughout the night). Although I had asked other doctors to cover for me, anything urgent involving my patients would still come through to me. The first day away from work was fantastic—the weather was beautiful, and we were outside relaxing as evening approached. And then my phone rang.

It was an intensive care unit doctor—an emergency evaluator for a transplant team. One of my patients had overdosed and was expected to die unless he received a transplant. The doctor explained that if the young man had overdosed as a direct effect of illness (e.g., if he'd taken too much medication because he was confused), he could get a transplant within hours. If he took the overdose as a suicide attempt, however, he wouldn't be eligible for the organ he needed to live. And because no one could know for sure, I was asked to give my best opinion about the cause of the overdose, and my opinion would determine what would happen next. The transplant evaluator reminded me that other people were in line to receive the transplant as well—people who very well might die without it.

I asked the doctor to give me twenty minutes to think about it, but I already knew the answer. My patient was very ill, and he'd tried to kill himself multiple times before. This sounded exactly like one of his suicide attempts.

While I was waiting to call the doctor back, my phone rang again. It was my patient's mother. I'd never spoken to her before, but she knew who I was, and she knew the situation. She hysterically begged me to tell the transplant team that my patient hadn't tried to kill himself, that this was a mistake on his part. She told me that my primary job was to help my patient and that if I told the transplant evaluator the truth, it would be as if I myself were killing her son.

A couple of minutes later, I called the doctor back and told her what I believed to be the truth. I've never been more torn between two responsibilities—the first to my patient and his mother, the other to the transplant team and whoever needed that organ. My patient died, and the transplant went to somebody else. I don't remember anything else about that vacation.

Most children grow up with ideas about who they'd like to be in the future—an astronaut, for example, or a teacher, or a firefighter—some role that creates a sense of pride, satisfaction, and importance. No child grows up fantasizing about being in so much misery and pain that they'll make multiple attempts to end their life in order to end their suffering. It would be unnatural, wouldn't it?

I think it's unnatural for adolescents and adults to think that way, too. I know we can't prevent it entirely, but we can sure do better than what we're doing now.

Another analogy for trauma is rain—endless rain. It might feel like a sprinkle at first, but with no protection we end up getting soaked to the bone, and the water just keeps accumulating all around us until we're carried away in a river of misery. That's what happened with my patient. This poor young man was pulled away by a torrent of suffering that he couldn't escape, a river of trauma swelling the banks before he was even born. I felt it, too. I was chest deep in it that day, but that's nothing compared to what it was like for his mother.

We can't turn a deluge of trauma into a drought overnight. But together we can help keep each other dry. Together we can find higher ground.

REFLECTION   Think about a time when you had to make a tough decision—one that affected the lives of other people in a profound way. How did your choice affect you? What trauma might you still be carrying from that time? What helps ease the pain of the decision you made?

CHAPTER 3

Shame and Its Accomplices

Trauma doesn't operate by itself. Regardless of the type, trauma gets a lot of help from a number of accomplices, chief among them shame. I think of shame as trauma's number one henchman—the thug who does the worst of the dirty work as well as the one who supervises trauma's other lackeys.

Think back to the four trauma vignettes at the end of chapter 1. Each involved a lot of difficult emotions and a sense of a changed world—elements of trauma that pave the way for shame. From the outside, it might seem obvious that the people involved (myself included) have little to feel ashamed about, but that's not what it usually feels like to the person experiencing the trauma. And unless a person consciously works to counteract shame, it will often do untold damage.

How many times have I heard people blame themselves for something they couldn't have anticipated or changed? How many times have I done the same? There are times when we as human beings really should have thought more clearly or planned ahead better, but usually we blame ourselves for situations beyond our control. It's often more difficult to understand the truth than it is to blame ourselves, and this is where shame likes to step in with all of its *shoulds* and *shouldn'ts*: "I should have known it was dangerous," "I should have told her I loved her more often before she died," "I shouldn't have done that," "I shouldn't be feeling this way," and so on.

I believe these shame-based thoughts arise from the feelings of hopelessness and helplessness that come with trauma. We want to change ourselves or the outside world, but shame misdirects us toward self-persecution, which does little to increase our competence or ability to make healthy decisions. We want to make the world a safer place to live in, but we have trouble distinguishing the best way to do so. Fortunately, suffering from trauma and its accomplices doesn't mean that we're actually hopeless or helpless. In this chapter, I want to introduce you to some of the *antidotes* I recommend for helping yourself and receiving the caring assistance of others.

A HEALTHIER YOU, A HEALTHIER US

Trauma and shame influence what we do to improve our lives as well as what we don't do. Do we choose to look for a better job? Leave an abusive relationship? Stop smoking? Eat foods that are good for our bodies? When shame is in play, the answer is more likely to be the less healthy option. Shame makes it way more difficult for us to have faith in ourselves or to have the confidence and self-love that remind us we deserve a good life. Perseverance and discipline are hard enough as it is without shame throwing additional obstacles in our path and sapping our ability to see the bigger picture.

To make matters even more challenging, the shame we experience as a result of trauma has an effect on the lives of others, especially those closest to us. Shame disconnects us from them, and our inner pain often turns into anger and frustration with others, especially when we're not taking good care of ourselves. In some cases, we don't limit the punishment just to ourselves, but we lash out at others in order to feel stronger and less vulnerable. This is where the *abuse begets abuse* adage originates. Of course, most people who suffer the trauma of abuse don't react by harming others, but it's no surprise that an abused person would experience intense anger and vulnerability and have trouble managing those feelings. That's why we need to do whatever we can to make sure those suffering from abuse are fully supported and met with compassion.

On a trip to the Andes once, I watched a master weaver create a vibrant tapestry. She drew together thick threads of seemingly infinite colors that appeared to spring out of one another and then lose themselves in the whole of what she was weaving on the loom, finding themselves again in the emergence of surprising new patterns. We're like that tapestry—interwoven in more ways than we can understand—and unlike it, too. We're different in that we're both the woven thing and the weaver, who's responsible for whatever emerges from the loom. Together, we're the artists who create the world we live in.

Simply put: A healthier *me* makes a healthier *we*, and a healthier we goes a long way to encouraging a healthier you. With this in mind, I offer the following antidotes to help us all heal from the trauma epidemic and kick its accomplices to the curb.

ACCOMPLICE   *Shame*
ANTIDOTE   *Uncovering Self-Talk*

Pay attention to the way you talk to yourself about yourself. You'd be surprised at how many people feel terrible about themselves without having any idea why. When I get my patients to examine their internal dialogue, they often report that they have a habit of repeating negative phrases to themselves—such as "I'm a loser" and "No one really likes me." Uncovering this type of self-talk might not make it change right away, but it's a good first step.

ANTIDOTE   *Reattributing Shame*

Whenever you start to feel ashamed about a traumatic event, ask yourself if the clothes fit. It might be true—especially in cases involving abuse—that *someone* should feel ashamed about it, but that person is likely not you. Shame has a way of convincing us to take the hit, but sometimes it's possible to reroute the attribution or at least not buy into what shame's telling us in the first place.

ACCOMPLICE   *Poor Self-Care*
ANTIDOTE   *Clarifying What People Deserve*

Write down the basics of what you think a person deserves in life—not you, specifically, but any person. Your list might include things like *three healthy meals a day, a reliable car*, or *not being scared at home*. Writing this out can help you discover whatever basics you might be lacking and give you some good ideas about what you can do to help yourself.

ANTIDOTE   *Describing What You Would Change*
If you had the ability to wave a magic wand and utterly change your life, how differently would it look? What things can you do to start making the changes you'd like?

ACCOMPLICE   *Risk-Taking Behaviors*
ANTIDOTE   *Reviewing Motivations*
Stop and think about why you engage in risk-taking behaviors. Is it to get hurt or killed? Is it to punish someone who has harmed you? Is it to punish yourself? Is it because risks are a distraction from something painful?

ANTIDOTE   *Investigating the Impulse*
Consider that you might be trying to prove something through your risk-taking. Whatever the behavior, investigate whether or not it involves proving something to yourself or someone else, even someone who isn't in your life anymore.

ACCOMPLICE   *Poor Sleep*
ANTIDOTE   *Relaxing Body and Mind*
Progressive muscle relaxation starts at your feet and moves up your body to the top of your head. It involves tensing individual muscles and then relaxing them, working your way up your body in a progressive fashion. This technique releases stress in your body wherever you're holding tension, and it can also inform you of tightness where you might not have been aware of holding it (which makes learning how to relax all the more important).

ANTIDOTE   *Employing Imagery*
For this antidote, I recommend using imagery that incorporates all five senses. For this reason, the beach is a popular choice. Seeing the water, hearing the waves, smelling and tasting the salt air, and feeling the sand all at once involves all of your senses and can guide your mind into a calmer, sleep-promoting state.

ACCOMPLICE   *Mood Decline*

ANTIDOTE   *Activating Body and Mind*

Continue to actively use your body and brain or increase your activity level if possible. Exercising, practicing fine motor skills, reading, and solving puzzles (crosswords, Sudoku, and so on) are all great ways to boost your mood.

ANTIDOTE   *Exploring Your Stressors*

It's often helpful to make a list of what's going right in your life as well as what's causing you stress. Often the latter list will provide the insight you need to find new routes to positive change.

ACCOMPLICE   *Anxiety*

ANTIDOTE   *Limiting Media*

A common cause of escalating anxiety is *news overdose*. More often than not, the news can feel like a sequence of harrowing stories, many of which are far too close to home. Limiting news intake by setting time limits or avoiding certain topics, for example, can reduce your baseline anxiety and tension to a more manageable level.

ANTIDOTE   *Identifying Triggers*

Look back to when your anxiety started to feel like more than you could handle. What was happening in your life at the time? Sometimes a seemingly minor event can turn out to have a big impact, and it often happens that something that doesn't feel like a big deal is the very thing that reminds you of something traumatic in your past. For example, a minor fender bender can trigger memories of a serious car crash in the past. You might walk away from the small accident just fine, but those triggered memories might be running around and around under the surface of your awareness, pumping out a flood of anxiety.

ACCOMPLICE   *Damaged Immunity*

ANTIDOTE   *Taking Care of Your Body and Mind*

Our immune system requires us to eat healthily, move our bodies, and get the proper amount of sleep. Even small improvements to your diet, exercise regime, and sleeping habits will boost your immunity.

ACCOMPLICE   *Nightmares and Flashbacks*

ANTIDOTE   *Seeking Assistance*

When you're suffering from any of trauma's accomplices, it's a good idea to ask for help from family, friends, and professionals. That being said, some antidotes are more effective than others. When it comes to the nightmares and flashbacks that accompany some types of trauma, I certainly don't recommend going it alone. Skilled psychotherapists are worth their weight in gold, and psychiatrists like me can recommend safe medical options that can help reduce the suffering from images and memories that can haunt us during waking hours or while asleep.

I Need to Learn from Him

When I was a psychiatrist in training, I was fortunate to have several outstanding supervising physicians. They came in handy when I was assigned the complicated patients who helped me learn the ropes of my trade—when to order a magnetic resonance image (MRI), for example, or how best to use certain medicines and other therapeutic techniques.

I was assigned a young man struggling to stop drinking. At the time, he was using alcohol in a life-threatening manner, whereas he'd been able to drink in moderation for a long time before this point. The fact was that he hated drinking—other than the occasional beer with the guys after baseball practice, that is. This man loved baseball.

He'd immigrated to the United States as a child, lived with his aunt and uncle, and found it difficult to fit in. His aunt and uncle did the best they could to help him, but he was shy and awkward, and he struggled. He was closest with his aunt, who beamed with pride at any and all of his accomplishments. She only spoke the language of the country she'd left a quarter-century before, and my patient used his English skills to help her navigate life in the United States.

Everything in his life changed when he discovered baseball in his teens. He had never tried it until a gym class forced everyone to learn the game and play different positions. Lacking both confidence and a natural physique for the sport, my patient anticipated feeling even more awkward and left out, but he was surprised to find that he was great at it. And it wasn't just that he was a hotshot on the field—he was also skilled at the planning and strategizing that go into baseball, and this allowed him to become a leader in the sport.

As a result, he gained the respect he had so badly wanted from his peers as well as attention from girls who'd never noticed him before, and all of these rewards made baseball even that much more fun. He was energetic and encouraging at practice, which enlivened the team and led to them winning more games. His aunt and other admirers often watched the team's practices and games from the stands, and he made them feel energetic and encouraged, too.

His self-confidence, social life, and career were coming along well, and he felt comfortable with his place in the world. This all changed abruptly when he contracted an illness that threatened his life. If that weren't bad enough, the illness impaired his physical coordination, and he could no longer play baseball. The man was crushed. He felt as if baseball had given him everything. What he didn't see was that baseball was just a vehicle that let him show everything inside of himself. He couldn't see that all of that leadership, intelligence, good-natured encouragement, and humor were his.

He was drinking to punish himself for being a failure. He considered his illness his fault, and he was using alcohol to hasten the end of his life. I felt completely incapable of helping him, but I had a particularly savvy supervisor—one who often saw solutions others didn't—and he made a profound suggestion that made all the difference. He simply said, "Let him teach you something."

I remember sitting in my office later that afternoon, thinking about the big picture I had missed. My patient felt ashamed, inadequate. And there I was—in his eyes, vigorous and healthy—trying to help him, but him having to see me was making him feel worse about himself. So I resolved to learn something from him—something he could feel proud of teaching me.

Several weeks later, he had taught me some words in the language he shared with his aunt. I could pronounce them well and even construct a few brief sentences. It wasn't easy, but I had benefited from his enthusiasm and encouragement, his ability to understand where I was having problems, and his skill at giving me just the right pointer here and there. I had benefited from his patience and sense of humor as well as from how good he felt when I got something right.

His aunt joined us for a session about eight weeks later. I was able to greet her in her own language, and my patient beamed with pride, even when I struggled. He tactfully helped me forward, and we felt like two young guys showing off for a respected elder who was proud of us both. She was especially proud of her nephew, who had taught his doctor something important. After that, we were finally able to decrease his drinking.

I had to learn from him. I had to let him help me. In the process, he was able to let me help him.

We each have so much potential within us. We each deserve the opportunity to explore our interests, learn about the world around us, and realize our potential. At the same time, we're all susceptible to shame, to becoming disheartened, to punishing ourselves when we deserve compassion, to giving up. We all need help sometimes, and there are times when any one of us could need that help desperately. The great news is that the most powerful helping tool at our disposal is real human connection, and it's a tool we can all hone and put to wonderful use.

❧ REFLECTION   First, think of a time when you quit doing something you loved because of shame or self-judgment. What was it like to lose that activity from your life? Then think of a time when the power of connection reminded you of some of your better qualities. Who helped you remember? How did they do it?

SHAME WORKS BEST IN THE DARK

I'll go into this more in chapter 11, but for now I'll just say that shame is an *affect*, and we have little choice but to experience affects. If someone were to jump in front of you and shove you to the ground, you'd probably feel afraid, angry, or both—but you'd experience those affects automatically before you even knew it. Your unconscious mind and your body know what's going on before you do, and they respond much faster than anyone could by choice. First the response and then the reflection.

Affects are meant to be powerful. They control us by elbowing in and pushing aside our ability to think and choose. From the perspective of evolution and survival, affects are meant to protect us, but they can also work against us in astounding ways, and shame works in one of those ways. Shame has the tendency to reshape our minds and our beliefs about ourselves and our world, and to do so in a hidden and secretive manner.

In chapter 1, I talked about how the official cause of death—the surface story—is often different from the actual cause—trauma. Sometimes, the real cause of death is what led to the cause listed on the official report. Sometimes, the real cause of death is the only reason there's a report in the first place. When this is the case, shame and its accomplices are always present. When people die in untimely ways, the *how* of their passing often has far less to teach us than the *why*. I assert that trauma is the why far more often than we recognize, and trauma is almost always accompanied by shame.

THE SECRET LESSONS OF TRAUMA

Children are constantly learning. If the lessons are strong enough, they etch themselves into our being and create the lenses through which we interpret the world. This happens when we're older, too, but in general, the younger we are, the deeper the etching and the more prominent the lens. We learn from what we're taught, from what we observe, and from what we experience. Here are some examples of how this plays out when it comes to trauma.

- A young boy runs to tell his father when he is proud of something. Sometimes his father smiles and says, "That's my son!" in response to the good grade or the goal scored, but sometimes his father pushes him away or even slaps him. The boy tries to figure out over and over how to get the good response and not the painful one, but what he doesn't know is that his father is an alcoholic. The boy learns that he can't control how his father responds to him—that he isn't good enough to consistently earn a good response and that he must be bad a lot of the time without even knowing it.

- A young girl is loved and nurtured at home, where she gets everything a child could want. But over time she learns that these things are not so good in the world outside of the home—her skin is a different color from that of the other kids at school, where she's told she eats weird food and wears strange clothes. Worse yet, no one wants to play with her, and the other children whisper about her and laugh at her outright. The girl tries to be nice and fit in, but nothing changes. And so she learns that all the good things at home are actually bad things and that she must be bad as well. After all, that's what everyone in the outside world thinks.

In these examples, the children carry the burden of believing that they are somehow bad, which results in a distorted view of themselves and the world that excludes opportunities and dampens the vibrancy of life. It's a lens that's been entirely distorted by shame.

- An adolescent boy doesn't have much at home, and his parents are constantly angry that they're poor because other people have taken all the good jobs. They say those people don't deserve to be here because they were born in another country and they believe things that go against the teachings of God. His parents deserve more, they say, and if they had it, they'd buy him the sneakers and the bike and the phone he wants, but they can't. The boy is bigger than the other kids at school, and it feels good to push them around and hit them, especially if they're from the families that shouldn't be in this country in the first place. He learns that he and his family are good but that the world isn't fair, and because the world isn't fair, his family doesn't get the good things they deserve. That makes it okay to push the other kids around, especially the bad ones.

Kids who grow up being told that they're better than others develop a lens that doesn't let in the suffering of others. And if they're informed that they're being denied the good things they deserve because they're persecuted, that lens will always be tinted with anger and also shame. The shame comes because they'll be more likely to get into trouble, perform more poorly in school, and therefore be identified as bad and problematic. And the belief in being persecuted can lead to persecuting others, which leads to more shame, which then furthers the feeling of being persecuted.

- An adolescent girl works hard and gets high grades in school. She plays sports and volunteers in the community. Her family and friends have always supported her and rewarded her with praise for these accomplishments, but lately her body has started changing. Now these changes seem to be all the kids at school care about. The group of girls she used to spend time with avoid her or make fun of her. Some of the boys say things she doesn't understand, and sometimes they grab her in places you aren't supposed to touch someone, and no one does anything to stop them. The girl learns that grades and sports and volunteering aren't all that important after all; or she learns that you can't trust the people you thought were your friends; or she learns that no one will protect you when people do things you don't like; or she learns that her body is bad; or she learns that she herself is bad.

Young people carrying the burden of being revalued for things that aren't about who they are or what they value can come to view the world through a lens obscured by confusion and disappointment. This makes it far more difficult for them to accurately assess and appreciate their identity and their qualities while generating further shame and despair.

- An adolescent boy works hard, gets good grades, and so on. But there's a new coach in his favorite sport who touches him in private places and tells the boy he'll be off the team if he doesn't keep it secret. When the man touches him like that, it gives him feelings and thoughts that are confusing and scary. He tries to make the coach happy in other ways—by practicing more and scoring more goals—but the touching doesn't stop. The boy learns that how hard he works at something doesn't matter and that he is bad for being so confused and scared. He believes the coach when he tells the boy that he's ungrateful for not appreciating how much attention the coach is giving him.

Young people traumatized by the abuse of a trusted adult can also come to view the world with confusion and disappointment. Abuse like this ensures that the lens through which they see the world transmits distorted information. It also sends back frightening and distorted images of the self—illusions constructed of shame and despair.

- A woman has worked and studied hard to get her dream job right out of college. She throws herself into her work, sacrificing time and sleep to achieve at a high level. She is out with colleagues after their first annual review, and she learns that several men achieving less than her have been given bigger raises. She talks to a few women who have been at the job longer than she has, and she's told that's just the way it is and not to make waves if she wants to move up in the company. She learns that hard work doesn't necessarily pay off after all. She stops trying so hard, she enjoys the work less, and her career suffers right along with her ambition.

A person demeaned and devalued in this way, especially while being informed that justice isn't achievable, can come to view the world through a lens cracked by disheartenment and disillusionment. The lens filters out light from which the person would otherwise receive nourishment and encouragement. Not surprisingly, this promotes shame as well because it conveys that the person was naive and gullible to have thought she was worth more in the first place.

- A man works in a factory where his father and grandfather worked before him, and he has risen to the rank of foreman. The factory's business has decreased over the past several years, and the man learns what he has feared but hoped would never happen—the factory is closing. He must continue working to support his family and is faced with three choices, none of which are good ones. He could move to a different town and find work there, take a lower-level job at another factory farther from his home, or go through a retraining program at a local community college. He learns that the times of his father and grandfather are over and that the world doesn't have much need for the skills he has to offer.

...ou found in your work with adults that—aside from certain traumatic ...—the patients with the worst problems suffered severe trauma in their ...ood?

...tely. But it's not just psychological, as if somehow that's not enough. ...ee it turn up in how their endocrine system is functioning and what ...pressed genetically. People are altered by trauma at that level, and ...something I don't think gets addressed enough. And then there's ...ue of generational trauma—kids being affected before they're even ...rom the trauma their parents or grandparents went through. ...ows up prominently when it comes to war. For example, all of these ... of my grandparents' generation in Germany who went through World ... and suffered terribly, whether it was in concentration camps, or they ...ortured, or they had to go through all of these horrible things just to sur-...nd then it was never spoken about. But you could see all of that trauma ...up in the generations after them—neurologically, genetically, and oth-... At the time, people weren't aware of consequences like these, but then ...elational issues show up down the line. Part of that is children grow-... being parented by traumatized survivors, which actually changes one's ...chemistry as well as the way certain genetic traits get expressed.

... we also see as the result of child abuse.

...right. Especially in the case of sexual abuse. I don't ever want to dimin-...e impact of other traumas on people, but I think the sexual abuse of ...en is probably one of the most brutal things that could happen to a ...a being.

...et there's still this common idea that trauma is something discrete, ...ited to the time when the event happened. It's almost as if we can ...ee it through a legal lens. Like, something bad happened at some ...in the past, where the trauma is sort of contained, but especially ...it comes to children, trauma isn't like that at all. It affects everything ...life going forward. What we don't get is that people are fundamen-...hanged by trauma. They're changed biologically. They're changed ...ns of gene expression and hormones and chemicals and neurotrans-...n, and that goes on forever. My hope is that people's notions of ...a catch up with the scientific research.

A person carrying the burden of being belittled and devalued while also feeling helpless can come to view the world through a lens that disperses the light and refracts the vitality of life. It's a lens that can make everything of value seem hopelessly far away, and it also promotes shame by making a person feel worthless.

The worse the trauma, the worse the cascade of harm that follows.

In each example above, there is a lesson—a secret lesson—that generates a host of extremely negative feelings. When we experience traumas like these, our views of who we are and how the world is shift in frightening ways cloaked in mystery. These secret lessons are most often learned alone, without being discussed with others or held up to the light of evaluation, and so we hold them deep within us. In trying to protect ourselves, we bury these things away from the world, the most harmful thing we could do to ourselves. And so we inadvertently plant and nurture the toxic seeds that we never asked for in the first place.

Shame tells us that we should never let these seeds see the light of day. Shame convinces us that we can't discard them because if we try, other people will see how terrible we are, and we'll be humiliated and exposed. This is how shame tricks us into planting the seeds of false lessons. Shame also tricks us into letting in its host of destructive accomplices, which together ensure that we nurture a toxic harvest of even more shame.

Trauma and the shame caused by its secret lessons hurt us all—every last one of us. At best, this hurt just results in decreased opportunity and less happiness. At worst, it's a wildfire that tears through our life. As a general rule, the worse the trauma, the worse the cascade of harm that follows.

Although shame is the primary negative affect I most often encounter in patients, anger, confusion, and frustration are prominent as well. It's typical for people to turn all of this pain inward, which gives rise to so many of the problems that plague us—drinking excessively, abusing drugs, ignoring medical issues, staying in harmful relationships, eating poorly, losing sleep . . . the list is endless. And then there are the problems that come from turning this pain outward—child abuse, rape, hate crimes, beatings outside of schools and bars, road rage, accidents from reckless driving. Again, the list is endless.

MY FAMILY'S EXPERIENCE WITH SHAME

After my brother died by suicide, my family faced three challenges—the first two were about grief, and the last one was about guilt and shame. We grieved for what my brother lost—all the milestones and life experiences he'd never get to have—but we also grieved for us. We missed him, and we'd go on missing him. Grief hurts like that, and that's natural.

The challenges of guilt and shame might be regular, but they're not natural. Trauma encourages us to scrutinize ourselves for what we should have seen or done differently, and it punishes us with harsh, unkind words on the inside. My family was no exception to this. My father was always more extroverted than my mother, so it was no surprise that he was able to stay more engaged in the world after Jonathan died and receive the support he needed. My mother, however, became more isolated, withdrawn, and depressed. I think this had everything to do with the unjustified guilt and shame she felt about Jonathan; I also suspect it paved the way for the cancer that took her life.

My other brother and I continued to strive and to move our lives forward. I can't speak for him, but some of my drive was reactive in that it came from a place of shame and inadequacy. On the outside, I was doing well in life, but my achievements couldn't mask my poor self-care, and on the inside, I was often a mess—insulting myself for every shortcoming and failure and making decisions that ensured I'd keep feeling bad about myself. I know firsthand how skilled trauma is at turning us against ourselves, and shame is one of its most effective weapons.

I'm in a much better place now, but it took a lot of vigilance and hard work. It also took a lot of skill and compassion from others.

A Converstaio[n
Stephanie zu Gu[

Several of the secret lessons discussed in
Plenty of excellent books have been w
trauma upon kids, and it's a topic that
we can give it. I want to offer something a little di
relying on the expertise of my friend Stephanie zu G

Stephanie is a dedicated advocate for childre
fighting child abuse in the United States, her hom
worldwide. In particular, she has extensive know
children face in the digital age, and she's tireless
these threats. She worked for a while as the presi
tion of Innocence in Danger, a nongovernmental
to the rights of children on the Internet and to r
child pornography. I asked Stephanie to talk with
as how trauma affects children, how racism and b
and how kids have been influenced by isolation in t

**Stephanie, you wrote a book about childhood tra
my knowledge isn't necessarily direct. Most of my w
I obviously know that childhood trauma paves the
but I'm not an expert on the specifics.**

A person carrying the burden of being belittled and devalued while also feeling helpless can come to view the world through a lens that disperses the light and refracts the vitality of life. It's a lens that can make everything of value seem hopelessly far away, and it also promotes shame by making a person feel worthless.

> **The worse the trauma, the worse the cascade of harm that follows.**

In each example above, there is a lesson—a secret lesson—that generates a host of extremely negative feelings. When we experience traumas like these, our views of who we are and how the world is shift in frightening ways cloaked in mystery. These secret lessons are most often learned alone, without being discussed with others or held up to the light of evaluation, and so we hold them deep within us. In trying to protect ourselves, we bury these things away from the world, the most harmful thing we could do to ourselves. And so we inadvertently plant and nurture the toxic seeds that we never asked for in the first place.

Shame tells us that we should never let these seeds see the light of day. Shame convinces us that we can't discard them because if we try, other people will see how terrible we are, and we'll be humiliated and exposed. This is how shame tricks us into planting the seeds of false lessons. Shame also tricks us into letting in its host of destructive accomplices, which together ensure that we nurture a toxic harvest of even more shame.

Trauma and the shame caused by its secret lessons hurt us all—every last one of us. At best, this hurt just results in decreased opportunity and less happiness. At worst, it's a wildfire that tears through our life. As a general rule, the worse the trauma, the worse the cascade of harm that follows.

Although shame is the primary negative affect I most often encounter in patients, anger, confusion, and frustration are prominent as well. It's typical for people to turn all of this pain inward, which gives rise to so many of the problems that plague us—drinking excessively, abusing drugs, ignoring medical issues, staying in harmful relationships, eating poorly, losing sleep . . . the list is endless. And then there are the problems that come from turning this pain outward—child abuse, rape, hate crimes, beatings outside of schools and bars, road rage, accidents from reckless driving. Again, the list is endless.

MY FAMILY'S EXPERIENCE WITH SHAME

After my brother died by suicide, my family faced three challenges—the first two were about grief, and the last one was about guilt and shame. We grieved for what my brother lost—all the milestones and life experiences he'd never get to have—but we also grieved for us. We missed him, and we'd go on missing him. Grief hurts like that, and that's natural.

The challenges of guilt and shame might be regular, but they're not natural. Trauma encourages us to scrutinize ourselves for what we should have seen or done differently, and it punishes us with harsh, unkind words on the inside. My family was no exception to this. My father was always more extroverted than my mother, so it was no surprise that he was able to stay more engaged in the world after Jonathan died and receive the support he needed. My mother, however, became more isolated, withdrawn, and depressed. I think this had everything to do with the unjustified guilt and shame she felt about Jonathan; I also suspect it paved the way for the cancer that took her life.

My other brother and I continued to strive and to move our lives forward. I can't speak for him, but some of my drive was reactive in that it came from a place of shame and inadequacy. On the outside, I was doing well in life, but my achievements couldn't mask my poor self-care, and on the inside, I was often a mess—insulting myself for every shortcoming and failure and making decisions that ensured I'd keep feeling bad about myself. I know firsthand how skilled trauma is at turning us against ourselves, and shame is one of its most effective weapons.

I'm in a much better place now, but it took a lot of vigilance and hard work. It also took a lot of skill and compassion from others.

A Converstaion with
Stephanie zu Guttenberg

S everal of the secret lessons discussed in chapter 3 involve children. Plenty of excellent books have been written about the impact of trauma upon kids, and it's a topic that deserves all the attention we can give it. I want to offer something a little different here on the subject, relying on the expertise of my friend Stephanie zu Guttenberg.

Stephanie is a dedicated advocate for children and is well known for fighting child abuse in the United States, her home nation (Germany), and worldwide. In particular, she has extensive knowledge about the dangers children face in the digital age, and she's tireless in her efforts to reduce these threats. She worked for a while as the president of the German section of Innocence in Danger, a nongovernmental organization dedicated to the rights of children on the Internet and to restricting the spread of child pornography. I asked Stephanie to talk with me about topics such as how trauma affects children, how racism and bullying affect children, and how kids have been influenced by isolation in the pandemic.

Stephanie, you wrote a book about childhood trauma, an area in which my knowledge isn't necessarily direct. Most of my work is with adults, and I obviously know that childhood trauma paves the way for adult distress, but I'm not an expert on the specifics.

Have you found in your work with adults that—aside from certain traumatic events—the patients with the worst problems suffered severe trauma in their childhood?

Absolutely. But it's not just psychological, as if somehow that's not enough. I also see it turn up in how their endocrine system is functioning and what gets expressed genetically. People are altered by trauma at that level, and that's something I don't think gets addressed enough. And then there's the issue of generational trauma—kids being affected before they're even born from the trauma their parents or grandparents went through.

That shows up prominently when it comes to war. For example, all of these people of my grandparents' generation in Germany who went through World War II and suffered terribly, whether it was in concentration camps, or they were tortured, or they had to go through all of these horrible things just to survive. And then it was never spoken about. But you could see all of that trauma show up in the generations after them—neurologically, genetically, and otherwise. At the time, people weren't aware of consequences like these, but then these relational issues show up down the line. Part of that is children growing up being parented by traumatized survivors, which actually changes one's brain chemistry as well as the way certain genetic traits get expressed.

Which we also see as the result of child abuse.

That's right. Especially in the case of sexual abuse. I don't ever want to diminish the impact of other traumas on people, but I think the sexual abuse of children is probably one of the most brutal things that could happen to a human being.

And yet there's still this common idea that trauma is something discrete, or limited to the time when the event happened. It's almost as if we can only see it through a legal lens. Like, something bad happened at some point in the past, where the trauma is sort of contained, but especially when it comes to children, trauma isn't like that at all. It affects everything else in life going forward. What we don't get is that people are fundamentally changed by trauma. They're changed biologically. They're changed in terms of gene expression and hormones and chemicals and neurotransmission, and that goes on forever. My hope is that people's notions of trauma catch up with the scientific research.

Especially when it comes to sexual abuse, people tend to be dismissive about the ongoing effects. For example, with child pornography, they'll say, "What's the big deal? It's just a picture," or "It's just a movie," as if the footage is something static that happened at some point in the past but is over now. They don't get what this type of abuse does to people. That also shows up when people question victims for taking so long to speak up about what happened to them. They don't understand that the trauma is so severe and the pain these people are feeling is so brutal that they can't remember events in typical fashion because their brain and their mental state has been working overtime to protect them from that pain. Fortunately, I've found that people are becoming more receptive to the latest data from epigenetics, for example. It's just that we haven't been informed of just how durable and pervasive the effects of trauma are, especially when it comes to kids.

I think shame plays a big role here, too. Trauma of all types tends to be accompanied by shame, so a lot gets internalized and legitimized because of that. And people don't talk about just how terrible their experience of the world is because of all this shame.

Perpetrators use that, too. And that's also what's going on when we blame the victims. Kids are sent back into abusive situations because their parents or caregivers aren't paying attention, and then the perpetrator says, "You must like it because you came back." So, on top of it all, the kids are being told that it's their fault.

And being taught that they're the one who's responsible for being abused in the first place. So shame just piles higher and higher. It's no wonder that people don't want to talk about being abused or that they don't seek help. And kids don't yet have the ability to see how messed up this is.

Again, that's how perpetrators like to work.

When we don't look at the biological changes created by sexual abuse, it's also a perfect setup for problems like depression, anxiety, and substance abuse. Think of all the subsequent problems driven by this, and the whole situation is almost perfectly created to make that person keep it all pent up inside.

And it's often that the worst cases are the ones we never hear about.

Because the more severe the trauma, the more shame there is to make people hide it. It's usually the opposite from what happens with medical conditions—the worse the rash or the pain is, the more likely people are to go get help.

In Germany, it's estimated that only one in every fifteen to twenty cases of sexual abuse is reported. So imagine how high the numbers really are. And there's this other idea that most of it happens to kids in lower-income situations, but that's not true. Some of the worst cases of abuse I know about involve a lot of wealth because it takes a lot of money and connections to keep things hidden and traffic children. How's a child supposed to escape a situation like that? Even in more typical situations, on average it takes a child reporting sexual abuse eight times before they're believed.

Eight times?

That's right. Imagine that. Approximately eight times a child has to ask for help because our society is inclined not to believe that sexual abuse is an actual thing. Perpetrators use this, which is why many of them like to get jobs with trusted access to children—priests and coaches, for example. And who wants to believe that kids are getting abused by priests and coaches? Or the leaders of youth camps? Perpetrators in these roles also don't just go out and abuse the kids right away. They build the relationship with the kids and their parents so that the parents and caregivers would never suspect them of harming their children. Not to mention that we're inclined to believe grown-ups much more than children, even though children aren't very good liars. You have to learn to do that over time.

I can't get over this idea of needing to ask for help eight times. Who does that, really? I mean, most of us give up asking for help after two or three times, tops. There are very few things I would ask for help about eight times, especially something with so much stigma attached to it. That certainly explains why only one in every fifteen to twenty cases comes to light. We have an entire social system dramatically predisposed to not knowing the truth of this.

I think we're a little more aware these days because of cases portrayed in the media, but there's still far too much sweeping it under the rug. You see that happen with religious institutions and schools. The people running those institutions and schools are very often more concerned with the scandal and the damage it would do than with standing up for the children. So even when it does come out that abuse has happened, often a lot of time has gone by, but the sooner we can step in to help, the better a child's chances are of healing.

So then we have the original trauma and subsequent traumas, too. For example, the trauma of not being believed or the trauma of being sent back into the abusive situation so that it happens again. Kids get the message that they're not safe anywhere—certainly not with the abuser, but also not with the adults who should be watching out for them and looking for the signs and listening to what these kids are saying. That's adding the trauma of neglect, and the same thing happens with less dramatic forms of neglect, too. The traumas just start to pile up on top of the kid over time. Is it any wonder that so many children grow up anxious or depressed or lacking in self-confidence? Or looking to substances to soothe the pain? This is what we're setting kids up for. When you look at how society thinks of trauma and abuse in particular, it's entirely predictable. We can do so much better in identifying abuse, minimizing its occurrence and severity, and helping children when it happens.

Absolutely. And we can apply that to other problems children are facing as well. Bullying, for example, online and otherwise. Or all the traumas that refugee children face. Thousands and thousands of kids fleeing their homes. What happens to them? Even if they ever arrive in a safe zone, who's helping them process the horrors they've experienced? There's that old adage that only the tough survive, but we never ask what it took for them to survive.

And what happens if they're not so tough? Do we just forget about them because they're not going to make it? That's abhorrent.

As if surviving was the only meaningful goal. It doesn't even take personal cost into account, not to mention the stress to families, communities, our health-care system. Even in the best of situations, refugees like the ones able to make it to Germany—to finally arrive somewhere that offers basic stability and a break from constant fear—even these children are deeply traumatized. Where does all of that go? With the world in the condition it's in, how likely is it that these kids are getting the psychological or psychiatric support they need?

Whatever's on offer is definitely paltry in comparison to the problem. And we're all hit with the fallout, no matter what the larger problem is—the pandemic, forest fires in the United States, or refugees from Syria as a result of political instability and violence. None of us is exempt. There's no class of person who's beyond this, and yet there's this idea that we can buffer ourselves and call it someone else's problem. But turning away from the glaring truth in front of us just creates more trauma.

Globally, we have chronically underestimated the importance of mental health, especially with children. I think the United States is a little further ahead than Germany in this regard because at least most kids have access to a school psychologist, but it's still nowhere close to what it should be. We should at least pay as much attention to mental health as we do to math, physics, chemistry, and language arts. Our emotional intelligence is lagging, and we can't expect kids to learn if we don't teach them.

Instead, we're teaching them—and I'm talking about US politics here—that success goes hand in hand with humiliating and insulting others. That bullying is okay.

Right. Instead of steering kids to greater emotional intelligence. But we could teach them from fairly early on not just that bullying is wrong but that there's a bigger picture. What's going on in that kid's life, for example? Why are they bullying in the first place? It's a way to learn about shame, feelings of inadequacy, and all this other stuff that goes on inside all of us. How does it feel when we lash out and treat someone else poorly? How does it feel when we don't act that way? We're not giving kids enough opportunities to learn what's constructive and what's not, not to mention what promotes well-being and self-confidence. And then what are children supposed to think when the people elected to be our country's leaders and role models act so terribly in public?

I do a lot of work with kids in digital education, especially about online shaming and bullying. We've done these experiments that young people know they are being monitored in which some of them are the designated bullies, some are the observers, and some are picked to get bullied. And the dynamics that show up are shocking. In-person bullying is one thing because you're there face-to-face, but with these online experiments, it quickly gets out of hand. The designated bullies really go for it and send all of these shockingly mean messages. Afterward, we get all the kids together and talk about it, and it's incredibly informative. They talk about how embarrassed they were to watch it all happen and how terrible they felt to receive and to deliver the bullying. It helps them understand digital citizenship in a whole new way, and it really has an effect on how they communicate online. It's a great example of what can result when you put resources into educating children about these larger issues. In this case, the kids know how to identify bullying, are more motivated to do something about it when they see it, and are way more mindful about the messages they send. That being said, it was a hard experiment to be involved with, and I don't really want to do it again.

I can see why. But there's certainly value in bringing light to a form of awfulness that usually takes place in the dark.
Everyone just felt terrible about it. The kids doing the bullying were really confused. It was as if they didn't know what was going on, and they were being carried away by this energy of bullying. They felt awful about themselves afterward.

I want to follow up on your work with digital citizenship. Can you speak to that more? I'd also like to hear your thoughts about more systemic issues such as racism and how that plays out online.
Sure. Well, most of us are aware that technology is developing incredibly quickly, and it's changed the world pretty dramatically over the past few decades. At some point in the future, you won't even be able to use your washing machine without your smartphone, and smartphones are going to look a lot different than they do right now. There's an exciting aspect to this, of course, because new technology means new possibilities, and untold options begin to open up. However, when it comes to the internet and virtual meetings during the pandemic and the overall prominence of social media in our lives, we're somehow losing touch with the rules and guidelines that govern our real-world, face-to-face interactions. Ideally, there shouldn't be so much difference between how I deal with people online versus how I deal with them on the streets. Most people would never think of insulting other people on the street—at least not out loud—or openly criticizing them for their skin color, culture, religion, or what have you. But the online world is turning out to be different.

There's this idea that it's not the real world. That it somehow has a whole new set of rules that are more permissive. And too many people are taking that as an okay to engage in inappropriate or just downright shameful behavior. But why should the rules be any different?

There's a huge difference between me and you sitting in front of each other versus us communicating over some sort of digital tool where it feels as if the distance between us is great. It's as if we're not interacting with people anymore, just staring into screens. And children are growing up like this more and more these days, which makes it crucial that we find ways to instill the basic rules of behavior in them. That's why digital education is so important.

Especially now, when more is happening virtually as opposed to in person. But we're still people, and we need to get clear about the realworld values we're invested in—civility, for example, or kindness and compassion. If those are actually our values, we need to accentuate them in virtual life, too.

Virtual technology is a tool, and like the other tools we've invented, we have to learn how to use it properly. A chainsaw has some beneficial uses, but it can also do some pretty horrible things. What we're doing online is still real; we're just using different tools to do it.

We also have these societal notions that play out online, too—things we have trouble acknowledging. For example, the idea that some people are more important than others, which is why I wanted to talk with you about digital citizenship and racism.

It's a complex topic because racism looks different depending on where you are in the world. Racism against people of color looks different in the United States than it does in Germany, where we've had our own brand of racism, and prejudice against Islam is a lot different in the Western world than it is elsewhere. But people who feel miserable about themselves sometimes use that by trying to make other people feel miserable, especially people they can scapegoat for whatever they think is going wrong in their lives. Leaders throughout history have taken advantage of this—Hitler among them. They recognize the misery that's going on and convince people to look outside of themselves for the cause. And when children grow up in households that tell them that other people—especially those of a different skin color—are the issue, that's hard to correct. It's much easier to point at someone else than to point at yourself. We typically don't like to own up to our own faults and mistakes, and that definitely shows up online.

Going back to the topic of emotional intelligence, we're not so great at educating children about their feelings. Why does a kid feel ashamed in the first place? What's going on that a child would want to make somebody else feel bad? If we don't look into it and answer questions like that, how can we possibly solve problems like bullying and racism?
Sadly, racism is deeply ingrained in our cultures, and I think the only way to change it is through education. As with sexual abuse, we need more focus on why it's happening and helping those who need help, and then we can start to build more positive messages around it. Sexual abuse is such a horrible thing to think about, and very few people want to talk about it, but if you frame it in terms of strength, something changes. No one's going to push back and say they don't want strong kids. So you work to raise strong kids—you strengthen their self-awareness, you strengthen their body awareness, you strengthen their boundaries and their power to say no. And you educate their teachers, parents, lawmakers, and judges, too. I think this is our only way forward, and I think it's the same approach we should take to racism. Children should know about racism from an early age—why it happens, why people do it, and what it does to the people who suffer from it.

That's how I think about trauma, too. Education is the most powerful anti-trauma mechanism we have. And the earlier we start, the better.
From early childhood. We've definitely found that to be true with kids and sexual abuse. We did a program with some young kids years ago in Berlin, and one of these boys later got lured into a situation with a perpetrator—he was nine or ten when this happened—and the boy loudly started shouting about child abuse and ran out of there, and his parents called the police. They took the perpetrator into custody, and the police asked the kid how he knew what to do because he really did everything right, and he said he'd learned it all from our school program.

That's a measurable triumph. The boy knew it wasn't normal, he knew it wasn't his fault, and he knew what to do about it—to leave the situation and get help. I want us to do that across the board. So that kids know that prejudice because of race or religion or country of origin or wealth

or whatever is wrong. Not only that, but they know how to respond to it. If we can educate kids early enough, what we're doing is building in these trauma-avoidance mechanisms so these kids grow up knowing how to respond, whether it's a pedophile trying to lure them away with puppies or an adult saying something racist or otherwise insulting. And then being in touch with their emotions in such a way that they can actually feel the emotional effects of what occurred, and know it doesn't have to do with them, but instead has to do with the other person. Proper attribution. What's wrong with that person as opposed to what's wrong with me. If we start early enough, we can make a huge difference. That's what I'm trying to do with digital education—working for long-term change for the generations to come. It's so hard to make substantive change in the moment, and whatever changes we can make don't happen very quickly, but we can positively influence these kids and that will make the difference down the road.

Right. And what bigger job do we have as adults than to protect children and try to make a better world for them—like one we feel okay handing off to them?
There's a quote I keep on my desk that says, "Let's raise children that don't have to recover from their childhood."

What bigger responsibility is there? Let's at least give them a world that doesn't feel terrifying to grow up in. Everything we're talking about involves mitigating trauma.
There are enough normal traumas in life as it is—accidents, people close dying—and we can't change that. But we can at least put systems in place that are helpful—systems that work right away when something bad happens. For me, schools are essential in this regard because we don't have a lot of say about what happens at home. We have the most connection to young people from all sorts of backgrounds in school.

As you say, there's plenty of hardship to go around as it is. Take the Covid pandemic, for example. Everyone's affected by it, but some countries are definitely taking care of their children better than others. I can't speak very highly of how we've managed the virus in the United States. In fact, I know we've added to the trauma with all of this political squabbling and

infantile indulgence. You've lived in both countries—what difference do you see between how Covid is being handled in the United States and how Germany is responding?

The most obvious difference is health care. Germany has a well-functioning health-care system, and most people are insured—they can get medical attention if they need it. That's not the case in the United States. The countries have also responded differently when it comes to school lockdowns. Germany is worse in this regard when it comes to digital education and keeping connected to kids that way, but in any case, I'm worried about the long-term effects of isolation and domestic abuse on the rise during lockdown—depression, anxiety, problems with the immune system, and so on. So that brings us back to health care. When that's lacking, lower-income families are hit the hardest.

I'm worried about how this is going to play out in the future. I mean, there's a pandemic going on, so we have to have lockdowns and quarantines, but how much worse are we making it? How much unnecessary trauma are we creating with our unhealthy responses and failing health-care system? And, like you said, people who are socioeconomically deprived are going to be hit the hardest because they were barely holding on in the first place.

People are losing their jobs in Germany, too. It's just that there's more support from the government.

Long term, I think we need to learn from that. We're going to have to live with this virus for a while and maybe others like it, but we're living in a world where things like this can happen, and we need to put reasonable safeguards in place. Maybe that comes down to more international and local public health-care mechanisms and communication.

And education. That's been a thread through our conversation today.

The earlier, the better.

Right. And not just on academic subjects but on all of these social and emotional aspects of life. That's building in those safeguards against trauma, like you said.

That emotional aspect has been a thread, too. Trauma is an emotional thing, and emotions drive so much of who we are.

That's the beauty of humankind—that we're emotional beings. We're steered by emotions.

And that's where trauma steps in. It doesn't matter whether it's from child abuse or racism or being shut off from other people during a pandemic, trauma twists those emotions and perceptions and actually changes how we experience the world. And ourselves. It can even alter memories into something they weren't before the trauma happened. A kid who was full of hope and light before being traumatized starts to feel terrible about themselves and sees the world as unsafe.

It's hard for any type of logical or rational thinking to overrule that. After that gets ingrained, it's hard to combat. That's why we have to intervene and start early with education and the safeguards we're talking about. That's what's going to win the day.

CHAPTER 5

Compassion, Community, and Humanity

Compassion, community, and humanity are intertwined in that they exemplify the full expression of who we are as humans. Although trauma can make us feel isolated and lonely, the truth is that we're all in this together. Compassion enables us to care about other people, to relate to them with kindness, and to consider the world from their perspective. Community is the embodied acknowledgment of our interdependence with other people—our behaviors affect one another. Finally, humanity is the recognition that—as people who share this world—all of us suffer. Furthermore, that suffering matters.

Compassion, community, and humanity are our birthright. For people, they're what make the world go round. They're also some of the first things to go when trauma finds its way into our homes.

We people have many homes, both literal and figurative—our actual abodes (for those of us privileged enough to have them), our bodies, and the minds and hearts of the people who love us and whom we love, as well as our larger communities, be they our neighborhoods, towns, countries, or planet. Trauma hides in each of these homes, camouflaged in ways to make it seem normal. We know there's something off with self-doubt and shame, for example, but after a while they just seem part of the texture of life—feeling bad about ourselves for one thing or the other becomes normal, we doubt ourselves when we most need to believe in ourselves, and we doubt others in this way, too.

All types of trauma can bring self-doubt and shame, which flow from the changes in our emotions and the altering of our memories (more on the way that happens in part III of this book). Self-doubt and shame amplify the impacts of trauma, leading to a terrible cycle that can escalate without anyone recognizing what's going on. As we saw in chapter 3, shame is typically a misguided sense of responsibility for awful things that have happened. Unfortunately, that misattribution can lead to self-neglect, self-punishment, and worse.

Honey, You're the First One Who's Noticed

Early in my career, I worked as a consulting psychiatrist in several nursing homes. Most of the work related to memory issues—trying to slow the progression of memory loss or treating the problems that follow it. On one routine consultation, I was asked to see an elderly woman successfully treated for cancer. Despite this, she had been losing weight rapidly over the previous few months. She was receiving medicines to help stop her weight loss but to no avail, and I was asked to assess whether she might be suffering from depression or some unrecognized effect of her cancer treatment.

As I looked over her chart, I was surprised at how good her labs looked. There was no sign of resurgent cancer or of any side effect from its treatment. I asked the nurses and nursing assistants about her, and they told me how sweet and kind the woman was and also about her remarkably sharp memory. I wasn't expecting this, and I was curious about what she would be like in person.

She was a jolting sight when I entered her room. She was terribly thin, wearing a sheer nightgown that revealed just how close to death she was. But she was bright-eyed, moved gracefully despite her condition, and was funny and quick-witted. She definitely didn't seem depressed, and I already knew there was no sign of cancer in her blood. I couldn't find any other medical explanation for her weight loss and increasing frailty and weakness. It didn't make sense.

Whenever we spoke of her family and interests, I noted that she was remarkably carefree and also that she expressed a lot of curiosity about me and my work as a psychiatrist. When it came to her weight loss, she seemed reflective and even expressed curiosity about what was happening to her body, but after a while the cause became obvious. She wasn't even hiding it; in fact, she was waiting to see if I'd discover it. We were sitting on her couch together when I said, "I understand. You're starving yourself." She smiled, took my hand in her own thin, fragile hand, and said in a charming, *now-you're-in-the-club*, confidential way, "Honey, you're the first one who's noticed."

Because she was so pleasant, no one ever suspected her, so it was easy enough for her to dispose of food and her appetite-stimulating medicines. In her mind, the success of her cancer treatment had been an unwelcome surprise. That's when she started taking matters into her own hands. "Why?" I asked.

She told me that someone had taken advantage of her financially, that she'd lost everything, and that she was finally owning up to her responsibility to her children and grandchildren—at which she was convinced she'd failed—so she was imposing a fatal penalty upon herself. She'd felt like a terrible burden to them, and the misery of that feeling was unbearable, so she decided to starve herself to death. At this point, she sweetly reminded me, it was too late—no matter how I assessed her, there was nothing anyone could do about it. She was resolved and at peace. Before I left, she thanked me for our conversation and invited me back to visit her again if she were still around.

It's terrible to believe that you've failed at a solemn duty. And the resulting shame can be excruciating. These are the times we need compassion the most, but shame can convince us to keep it at bay even when we'd never hesitate to offer compassion to others in the same situation. In these circumstances, we can become desperate to gain any sort of foothold or sense of control, and sometimes that control shows up in self-destructive ways.

I think that's what this woman was going through. I think her internal battle with shame led to the secret she was keeping from everyone, but the life force inside of her was too strong to go through it utterly alone. In her final days, she invited me to share her secret and to create a few moments of real human connection.

🦋 REFLECTION   Think about a time when you felt convinced you'd let someone down who was very close to you—someone who depended on you. What feelings of shame did you experience? How did that shame affect how you acted toward yourself and those who love you? How did that shame alter your experiences of compassion, community, and humanity?

TRAUMA CHANGES THE MAP

The world is far too short on compassion, community, and humanity, but people aren't—at least, not when we're born. We all have the capacity for them; it's just that trauma stunts them, grinds them down, or hides them from us entirely. It's like we're given a map of life at birth—with paths going out in various directions. All of these journeys lie in front of us, and various features of the terrain can make travel difficult—unscalable mountains, canyons, deserts, and oceans we can only cross with the help of others.

Despite the traumas we face, we must take better care of ourselves and in the process take better care of others.

But trauma comes along and changes the map. It scratches out some of the nicer destinations. It draws up swamps and thorny spots in places that were once safe. It makes life look like there's no way we could ever get to the coast and cross the water to see what's on the other side. In effect, trauma makes us forget the map we were born with and convinces us the marred map was there all along. Before trauma came along, the features of the terrain that can make travel difficult were just another part of the journey. After trauma, they're often all we can see (and most of them aren't even real).

When our lives become limited in this way, so do our capacities for compassion, community, and humanity. None of these can flourish when we're confused and afraid and feel convinced we're alone. For this reason, self-care is paramount. Despite the traumas we face, we must take better care of ourselves and in the process take better care of others.

Uncle Rango, the War Hero

My Uncle Rango grew up in the Italian immigrant section of Trenton, New Jersey, in the 1920s and 1930s. He was part of a big family trying to survive during difficult economic times, and he had to become self-sufficient at an early age. He was not the best student, and his formal education ended during middle school after a fight with one of his teachers. So my uncle took a job in a sweltering bakery, and then he was drafted into the US Army during World War II. He was shipped off to Europe and sent to the front lines.

My uncle initially served as a mechanic's assistant, but he began to rise through the ranks as the Allies fought their way through France and into Germany. Uncle Rango was recognized as being shrewd, brave, and capable of effective strategy in the middle of chaos and carnage. At one point, his company became trapped behind enemy lines, and the officers were killed in combat by the overwhelming opposition. Over the radio, my uncle was elevated in rank and put in charge of the dwindling group of remaining men. No one expected them to survive.

Uncle Rango led every one of those men out without losing a single American life.

Whenever my uncle would tell me this story, he'd become upset—he even seemed ashamed at times. I couldn't understand his reaction, which was strikingly atypical of him. He was kind and jovial, but his inner strength (as well as his physical strength) was unmistakable. After the war, he'd made a career laying tile, and the work kept him robust. We all knew that the war had shaped his character, but he was almost always composed, and seeing him upset and ashamed was more than unusual. The more

I listened to his stories, however, the more subtleties I found in them—Uncle Rango was ashamed about something, but he was also proud. It was complicated.

Here's the thing: Uncle Rango was able to lead his men out, but it required great stealth and silence while moving through the night. The Americans also had three German prisoners of war with them. My uncle knew he wouldn't be able to bring the Germans along, and he also couldn't leave them behind. Enemy soldiers were all around them, and either option would result in the Americans being discovered and likely killed within the hour. Uncle Rango knew that any responsible person in his position would have the three German soldiers executed, but he also felt it would be immoral to ask one of his men to do it. That's why he shot the Germans himself.

It haunted him the rest of his life. He said they were just kids— just like the Americans. But he also knew that killing the captured soldiers was the only way he and his men were able to escape.

After the war, Uncle Rango received letters from several of his men for the rest of his life. They wrote to him whenever something important happened in their lives. One of the men went on to have a large family, and he wrote Uncle Rango after every child was born and then also years later after every grandchild and great-grandchild was born. In those letters, the man reminded Uncle Rango that none of these people would be alive were it not for what he'd done during the war.

Uncle Rango told me that the best and the worst sometimes come together, that you might someday have to do something terrible in order to do the right thing. He said he was sure he did the right thing despite how much it still troubled him. My uncle was decorated for his heroism for leading the men to safety, and also for his choice during another battle in which he left a foxhole under heavy fire to rescue an injured soldier. He valued this latter decoration more because it was uncomplicated. Nothing haunted him about saving that man.

Uncle Rango's war trauma left him not only with lifelong shame but also with a sense of pride and hard-won achievement.

Despite having to do something no person should ever have to do, my uncle went on to lead an industrious and happy life with my Aunt Rose. The two of them were dedicated to each other throughout decades of marriage, and I believe one way he kept going forward despite his trauma was because of her love and how she always considered him a war hero for enduring the unimaginable in order to protect her and our country. After my uncle died, Aunt Rose burned all of those letters. They were for him, she said, and not for anyone else to read. When Aunt Rose died, she was buried with my uncle's US Army dog tags.

REFLECTION Think about a time when doing the right thing also meant doing something truly difficult. It needn't be an act that left you with feelings of shame, just something in which—as Uncle Rango said—the best and worst came together. How does it feel to reflect on it now? What helped you make sense of the experience? Who supported you as you dealt with the complex set of accompanying emotions?

Despite our trials and traumas, we all have the capacity for compassion, community, and humanity. Few of us have had to make the kind of choice Uncle Rango did, but most of us live with the legacy of trauma in one way or another. The choices we make when faced with that legacy matter—they matter to us, of course, but they also matter to other people and often in ways we could never imagine.

Trauma isn't the last word.

One of my most favorite words is *generative*. It means creating something valuable or adding to the world in a positive way. Being generative can take the form of saving soldiers during a war or building a bridge or inventing a vaccine for a terrible virus, but for most of us, being generative is a lot more likely to take the form of a smile to a stranger, a supportive word to a friend in trouble, or helping the elderly couple that lives next door. Compassion, community, and humanity require that we're as generative as possible.

It's not easy because trauma works against us, and the suffering that results from trauma changes the lens through which we see the world. In effect, trauma changes us and too often in ways that eat away at our sense of well-being as well as that of others. So much of this book sounds the alarm about trauma and making sure that people finally understand just how daunting an enemy it is. That being said, trauma isn't the last word. It's not omnipotent, and it's not fated to beat us.

We can understand how trauma takes hold, how it hides, and how it strikes. We can learn to recognize it, to call it out, to counter its strength, and even to prevent it from striking ourselves and our loved ones further. The ultimate goal is to prevent trauma in the first place, although it's just as important to heal the trauma that's already occurred—the trauma that's already within us. This means healing ourselves, but compassion, community, and humanity are also about healing others. The two efforts aren't separable; in fact, they're interdependent.

PART TWO

THE BIG PICTURE—
THE SOCIOLOGY OF TRAUMA

Leila was sure if her partner didn't come and she had
to listen to that marvelous music and to watch the
others sliding, gliding over the golden floor, she would
die at least, or faint, or lift her arms and fly out of
one of those dark windows that showed the stars.

KATHERINE MANSFIELD, "HER FIRST BALL"

CHAPTER 6

The Problems with
Trauma and Health Care

Of course, compassion, community, and humanity don't simply come down to our individual choices. The social systems that affect all of us either promote well-being or they don't, and this is no truer than when it comes to health care.

Astronomical brainpower and resources have been committed to the health-care industry. This has led to incredible advances in science, and the health-care industry has become quite adept at using this science to solve acute and often straightforward problems. That being said, trauma isn't straightforward, and it isn't a "problem" in the normal sense of the word—as you've learned in part I of this book, trauma is more akin to a web of interconnected problems.

Despite the innumerable people who work in health care who are intelligent, highly skilled, and compassionate, the health-care industry is not. In fact, as far too many people have experienced, the health-care system often feels more concerned about serving itself than the actual people who come in seeking help. When I first made the career shift to medicine, I expected health care to be organized with patients in mind and to be designed such that people are placed first and foremost. Wow, was I ever surprised.

I want to be clear that what follows in this chapter isn't a critique of my teachers or the institutions where I was educated and trained but, instead, of the health-care infrastructure, the overwhelming influence of the insurance industry, and a tradition steeped in shortsighted goals that prioritize efficiency and money over patients.

Vomit Bag

Hospitals are full of protocols. Protocols can be necessary and useful, of course, but they shouldn't be a substitute for what it takes to actually help people. I remember one protocol that applied to patients with eating disorders—we were supposed to lock their bathroom doors so they couldn't sneak in and purge. As if that measure would prevent them from purging elsewhere.

One day, I was assigned a new patient who had an intense delusion about needing to purge; otherwise, the mice who lived inside of her would chew their way out through her stomach. Understandably, she had a problem with the locked-door protocol. She came to us believing that not purging would equate to a terribly painful death involving rodents, so I reasoned that we could build some rapport first and find a way to intervene as she gained a little ground with treatment. She was angry and loudly adamant that we not lock her bathroom door, so I promised her we wouldn't. After some initial suspicion, she took me at my word, and this opening gesture of trust between us even resulted in her taking some helpful medicine.

Later that night, someone else on staff noticed that the protocol was not being followed, changed my orders, and locked the woman's bathroom door. No one contacted me about this; they just did it. Here's what happened next:

I went to visit her the next morning without knowing that someone had changed my order. The first thing I noticed was that the woman looked incredibly angry. The next thing I saw was her picking up a paper grocery bag that looked as if it were full of something wet because the bag was soaked and leaking. Then she swung the bag full of vomit and hit me with it. Terrified by what she'd done, she ran out of her room with a high-pitched screech. I screeched myself, disrobed in her bathroom (after finally getting it unlocked by one of the staff members), and showered off the vomit.

There's humor in getting hit with a bag of vomit, but the truth is that the whole event traumatized us both. I went back to work in scrubs and was shaking for the rest of the day, and the woman never trusted me again. She had to be transferred to someone else's care and had to suffer from increased security and even more restricted freedoms for what the hospital deemed an assault on her doctor.

Other than pointing out how protocols don't always allow for common-sense modifications, I guess the lesson here is that we can sometimes be perfectly well-intentioned and still create trauma for others. That's important to remember because when it comes to helping others, we have to be more than just well-intentioned. We have to understand who people are, what their particular life situation is, and if our help is more likely to do good than harm. This is doubly true when our actions inadvertently generate fear because it can cause people to express themselves in irrational and aggressive ways. In this way, fear creates more trauma just as trauma creates more fear.

◄REFLECTION Recall a time when you tried to help someone but ended up unintentionally harming them in the process. What did you learn from that experience? What guidelines were you following that didn't serve you or the other person? What would you do differently if offered a do-over?

Trauma naturally falls into the realm of mental health care, but that is just a system within the larger health-care industry, and it is no less susceptible to the problems that occur everywhere else in that industry. For example, mental health care is overly concerned with putting people into categories. Too often, practitioners with limited time make a list of a patient's symptoms only to figure out what bucket the person fits in. This is kind of like reading the ingredients of a baking recipe and then deciding what the end result is going to look and taste like. Flour, sugar, oil, water . . . must be a cake! If it's a cake, it's supposed to have frosting. And if the cake tells you it's a waffle, that's the cake's problem—put frosting on it anyway.

Again, this isn't to criticize practitioners simply doing the best they can within an imperfect (and sometimes harmful) system. Most doctors, nurses, and therapists know full well that people deserve to be treated better than baking products. They know that a handful of surface-level coping tactics aren't going to do the trick when it comes to trauma, and they're fully aware that the latest-and-greatest medicines they're being encouraged to give aren't all that different from the old ones and that they certainly aren't worth the new price tag. My critique is more for a system that requires its employees to prescribe insurance-approved Band-Aids for problems that require much more than Band-Aids, the same system that's more concerned with its big book of diagnoses than it is with actually helping people.

Among other detrimental results, the insurance and health-care industries have made it such that health-care practitioners have become afraid of their patients. We're afraid of their needs, afraid of their suffering, afraid they won't get the help they need, and afraid that it will all come back on us. This is what comes from assembly line medicine, and it's exhausting and unsatisfying to everyone. Health-care workers are given just enough time to recognize a patient's basic needs while the next one is already in line, all while onerous paperwork continues to pile up. In particular, doctors don't get the time they need to really get to know people, but you'd think such knowledge would go a long way toward actually helping them. And who wants to feel the suffering of one more person you don't have the time to get to know? You might as well do the paperwork right there in front of them, especially when your fifteen minutes are almost up.

It's not helpful to rely upon an arbitrary measure that wasn't exactly designed to help patients in the first place.

Despite this, the industry has insisted on relying upon satisfaction surveys. Just how satisfied are these patients supposed to feel? It's as if the whole culture is utterly oblivious to what health-care practitioners are trying to accomplish in the first place. I was once contacted by a hospital administrator who informed me of the very serious news that I had two abysmal survey results. One was from a patient who had overdosed and nearly died. He wanted his drugs back upon discharge from the hospital and was angry when I ordered them destroyed (standard practice, by the way). The other was from a patient suffering from severe paranoia who insisted I had lots of bodies buried in my backyard, all the more unlikely because I didn't have a backyard—I lived in a condo. And then there was the time the unit on which I worked received low scores for visiting-hour convenience. Our hours were twenty-four/seven.

I'm not suggesting we do away with oversight because it's certainly necessary, especially in health care. I'm just pointing out that it's not helpful to rely upon an arbitrary measure that wasn't exactly designed to help patients in the first place. And complaints like the ones mentioned above can also affect compensation, create needless hassle, and sometimes pose serious risk to health-care workers. Medical boards are known to be persecutory, and they are often empowered to flout due process with no accountability whatsoever. Although this might not be the standard outcome of an invalid or minor complaint, unjustified hassle and tremendous expense are fairly common, and far too many careers have been ruined for no valid reason.

Mental health practitioners are even more susceptible in this regard because the issues at hand are so deeply personal, intimate, and at times unpredictable. Any additional cautionary fear is antithetical to the personal connection required for us to make any meaningful difference. The human-to-human element is nowhere more important than when a person is sharing details of their inner thoughts and feelings—we absolutely must allow ourselves to be vulnerable if we are to explore and improve our mental health. Unfortunately, the systems in charge of providing mental health care prioritize minimizing costs, saving time, and "serving" as many patients as possible. Is it any wonder so many practitioners are harried and burdened with excessive workloads? And how many abandon the business of helping others simply because they aren't given the support they need to actually help patients heal from their trauma?

THERAPEUTIC ANTIDOTE: WHAT TO LOOK FOR IN A THERAPIST

I believe mental health care, like so much else in society, has trended toward simplistic solutions to complicated problems. Unfortunately, this means people often place hope in proposed solutions that turn out to be little more than window dressing. Psychotherapy can offer rich and rewarding change but only when it's done thoughtfully. The best therapy involves rapport and trust and time, and popular short-term solutions are often just one more way to kick the can down the road for the patient to deal with later. This won't do. So, when it comes to healing from trauma, I offer the following guidelines for anyone seeking help from a psychotherapist. If nothing else, maybe they will offer a reasonable standard of expectations that will help you to better advocate for what you need.

- **EYE CONTACT.** This might seem like a no-brainer, but you'd be surprised. Among other things, eye contact from a therapist lets you know they're interested in making an actual connection with you.

- **EXPRESSION OF INTEREST.** Eye contact will help you determine whether the therapist is genuinely interested in you and your suffering, but body language and the words they use will also cue you in.

- **EMPATHY.** This can be tricky because it isn't the therapist's job to feel your trauma to the degree you do. Look for signs of empathy but also for the lack of it. How distant does the therapist keep themselves from you? Are they reserved or engaging?

- **FOLLOW-THROUGH.** Does your therapist remember what you shared in the last session? Do they take an ongoing interest in your issues? If they say they'll look into something for you or learn more about something relevant to your care, do they? These are some other ways to determine whether the therapist thinks of you as a real person with a real life or merely as an entity who exists only within the appointed time of the session.

- **AN UNDERSTANDING OF THE PRACTICAL.** Does the therapist pay attention to the practical aspects of your life? Do they have a workable understanding of your circumstances? For example, do they know what it would mean for you to leave one job for another or end a triggering relationship? Can they distinguish between symptoms of a diagnosis and the effects of actual events and people in your life?

- **AWARENESS AND RESPECT FOR THE IMPACT OF YOUR TRAUMA.** It's not unheard of for therapists not to be sufficiently trauma informed. The idea that we can simply get over difficult things that happened to us in the past is far more common than it should be, and in my opinion, some popular cognitive-behavioral therapy (CBT) techniques perpetuate this notion. Beware of any therapeutic tools meant to soothe distress without also addressing the root issues of your trauma. An attachment to short-term measurable outcomes can be a sign that your therapist is beholden to an insurance-driven modality of care.

A patient once told me that any doctor who tried to help them without sharing a part of themselves could go to hell. I think a lot of us feel this way. It doesn't help our trauma to be seen as a thing, as just another problem to be quickly shuttled out of the office. We need doctors to treat us like kindred humans; we need them to be real with us. I don't think anyone who chooses to enter the healing professions does so with the goal of hiding from the people we're committed to helping. I truly believe most of us aspire to ease human suffering, but the health-care system—including mental health care—fails to foster and support this aspiration.

Doc, I'm Dead, and You're a Busy Man!

When I was still in training, I took care of a man sure that he was dead. I don't mean metaphorically, or in any joking manner, or even as a way to express hopelessness. He was sure—100 percent sure—that he had died and that his body had not yet caught up with his death.

He was extremely considerate for a dead person. He tolerated my physical examinations with the gentle protests of someone who knows the other person is doing something ridiculous—for example, physically examining a dead man to make sure nothing is wrong. I think he felt sorry for me and thought I didn't know any better. He'd say things like, "All those years of medical school, and here you come to examine a dead man?" and "When will you learn that I'm already gone?" and "When everyone wises up and puts me in the morgue, are you still going to come trying to listen to my heart?" He was being funny, but he really did think he was dead.

We liked each other a lot. We got along well, and I tried fruitlessly to help him. Medicines and therapy are like spitballs versus a tank when it comes to *Cotard's syndrome* (yes, it actually has a name). The diagnosis can present in different ways, but being convinced that you're dead is the textbook presentation psychiatrists learn about in school but so rarely actually see.

He felt guilty taking up my time. Once, in the most kindly of frustrated manners, he said emphatically, "Doc, I'm dead, and you're a busy man!" For the most part, he'd been accepting care only because he was afraid of getting me in trouble if he refused. As pleasant as I found him, the man had no friends or family, and he'd been living by himself, isolated, on a meager pension. He had a personality that liked to laugh and kid around, and he was an all-around nice guy, but there was nowhere for any of that to go. And no matter what I did, he was still convinced he was dead, and the hospital discharged him to believe he was dead all by himself at home.

His history was unclear, and I wasn't able to identify any substantial trauma. But aloneness on its own can be traumatic, and maybe if you live in this world long enough without meaning anything to anyone, you might just come to believe that you're already dead.

Have you ever felt so lonely or depressed that you were convinced you didn't matter to anyone? What supported you through that experience? If you've ever felt that your life didn't matter, what did other people do to help you feel otherwise?

The health-care system doesn't seem to care much about what happens to patients outside of the hospital or clinic, and it doesn't do that great a job when they're inside, either. While in training, I once worked at a *medication-only* clinic, where the idea is to maximize the prescribing ability of doctors and leave therapeutic interventions to less costly employees. Clinics such as these are set up for maximum throughput, with long wait times and shoddy communication among clinicians. I once worked with a young woman suffering from panic attacks—often addressed quite successfully with medicines—but she wasn't responding as expected. In fact, she was getting worse. She insisted she was taking the medicine as prescribed, and it began to dawn on me that something else was going on. I broke with the clinic's guidelines and spent the next appointment just talking to her, and she responded by opening up about the physical violence that awaited her at home every night. She was having panic attacks because she was living in constant fear, and the solution wasn't getting the right medicine, it was getting out of that situation (which I was able to help her do).

Maximum throughput clinics aren't set up for this. Seeing the big picture and not just focusing on alleviating symptoms seems like common sense to most of us but not to the system. Especially when it comes to health care, patients are shuttled in and out with little intervention when it comes to traumatic environments more likely to be the issue in the first place. Few people are able to get a grasp on their trauma while they're in the middle of experiencing it.

The Revolving Door

At a different time, I worked on a psychiatric unit with a young woman who was a *frequent flyer*—meaning that she came in and out of the unit regularly for the same reason. She'd been abused as a child and had experienced homelessness in her teens, which led to more abuse as well as drug use. She also had a couple of children, but their whereabouts were unknown to her and to us. For someone in her situation, drugs are an understandable choice.

Despite their consequences, drugs provide at least some short-term relief, and they're often used as a form of self-punishment or as a way out of life that isn't quite the same as directly killing yourself. They're also readily available and much easier to obtain than reliable shelter, safety, and nutritious meals. This woman was using drugs to self-soothe and self-punish, and I didn't blame her. She wasn't taking drugs for the sake of partying; she was taking drugs because she was beyond desperate.

Our health-care system has little to offer someone like this. As a nation, we end up spending enormous amounts of money for ER visits and hospitalizations, but we don't put our resources where they can actually matter. The only thing this woman received when she left the hospital was a voucher for a few days at a motel—the same motel that was a drug den and a beacon for predators. It wasn't that the social workers on the psychiatric unit weren't doing their jobs; it's that this was what the system was giving them to offer. Invariably, the woman would find her way back to us, back on street drugs and off her medicines, agitated and confused. She might leave the hospital in a slightly better state, but we couldn't give her a safe place to live or send her back to school or offer her a job.

Eventually, while out on the streets and off the medicines that prevented her from experiencing delusions, this woman attacked someone with a knife. The other person wasn't hurt, but they easily could have been. The story made the local news, and the picture they always used was of the woman at her worst—disheveled and distressed, almost inhuman looking. Time and again, that's the story the media feed us. This young woman was portrayed in the worst possible light—sinister and depraved—not someone suffering day in and day out from the ravages of childhood trauma, but as one of *them*. She was just another face of the inhuman people we good citizens are encouraged to pin our problems on.

I'm not saying she doesn't bear some responsibility. I'm saying that blaming societal ills on people like her will ensure that these cycles of violence and misery continue. We ignore these cycles at all of our peril. Trauma in childhood can lead to homelessness and sickness, and homelessness and sickness beget more trauma. This cycle fosters drug abuse, which adds fuel to an already dangerous fire and sometimes burns an innocent bystander like the person attacked with a knife. As the flames rage in a person like this woman, society offers the illusion of caring, but what's on offer isn't actually designed to make much of a difference. We tell ourselves that it can't be helped, and anyone who's spent time in crowded ERs or psychiatric wards knows just how cynical those places are. And they're the places where the people who need the most help show up.

❦REFLECTION   In part, this story is about how a broken system fails to help the very people it purports to assist. But it's also about a real person—a young woman whose childhood suffering led to a life with very few healthy options and who became just another societal scapegoat for her actions. What can we do for such people? What changes do we need to make as a country to prevent this? How could we better allocate our precious resources?

Unless society heals the health-care system, the health-care system will never be able to heal society. Nor will it stem the rising tide of trauma. We should at least be as aware of trauma as we are of climate disruption, air pollution, and other significant public health issues (the race for a workable vaccine in a pandemic, for example). What if we screened for trauma the same way we screen for vision and hearing problems? For scoliosis and cavities? How loud does the alarm have to be until we actually do something about it?

CHAPTER 7

A Conversation with
Daryn Reicherter, MD

Understanding what trauma does to individual brains and describing how this affects societies across generations requires extensive experience and research. It calls for people with expertise that spans the disciplines of medicine, law, and social sciences, and my friend Daryn Reicherter is such a person. He's a clinical professor of psychiatry and current director of the Human Rights in Trauma Mental Health Laboratory at Stanford University. Daryn is an expert in the area of cross-cultural trauma psychiatry, having spent more than a decade dedicated to providing a combination of administrative and clinical services in trauma mental health locally and internationally. Pertinent to this particular conversation, you'll learn that Daryn has developed new methods for using the mental health outcomes of human rights violations to produce advocacy, policy changes, and treatment for survivors. On the local level, he's also been heavily involved in creating mental health clinics in the San Francisco Bay Area for refugees.

Among other topics, I asked Daryn to talk with me about how our brains change after trauma, epigenetics, and how individual trauma shows up in the larger context of society.

If you don't mind, Daryn, could you start off by saying a little bit about you and your work these days?

Sure. I'm a clinical professor of psychiatry at Stanford, and most of what I do there involves working with trauma. I am the director of a practical lab about law and trauma in which we look at the psychological aspects of what happens to people who are traumatized and put that information forward to help with policy. One way this occurs is through informing court decisions with our research, which helps advocate for people who have survived extremes of trauma. I'm also the medical director of the Center for Survivors of Torture. So, in one venue, I'm mostly writing and advocating, and in the other I'm actually treating patients, mostly refugees who have survived unspeakable traumas.

You also work at the Stanford Center for Human Rights, correct?
That's where the lab is. The Stanford Center for Human Rights has a couple of different functions, and my lab is a large function in that program. "Interdisciplinary" has become a buzz term that people like to use, but that's really what the lab is all about—half of the faculty members are lawyers, and half are psychiatrists or psychologists. And then we have all the students and other people interested in human rights from various fields. For example, one of our partners is a journalist who writes advocacy pieces about human rights. So we've got true interdisciplinary input from the Human Rights Center, the Law School, undergrads, the School of Medicine, and so on. It's not like it used to be when the focus of labs tended to be so narrow, which makes ours quite interesting.

That means you have these incredible resources to draw from. For example, if you need to consult a pediatric endocrinologist or assess some legal policy as it pertains to refugees. The type of resources your lab has on hand is really unusual.
That's right. We were working in Haiti with women who'd been sexually violated, and we were attempting to get them humanitarian help by using psychiatric diagnoses like PTSD, but it wasn't working—the cases were taking way too long. But we were finally able to make it happen by having our ob-gyn partners review these women's medical records, and that's not something we could have done otherwise. We were able to get the women out right away because we could show that they needed medical care and that they couldn't get it where they were. That's what can happen when you have all of these different people involved.

Like six degrees of separation, almost.
Or fewer. In the world of human rights and trauma, it's sometimes only two or three degrees of separation. Having those connections makes all the difference. The reason the lab got involved in Iraq is because one of my colleagues knows the special advisor to the United Nations Secretary Council and thought we should work together on the Accountability Project for Iraq. And here we are—a year and a half into that project.

Normally there's just so much bureaucracy to deal with, but you're able to expedite work that might otherwise take forever. That's a huge deal when it comes to trauma, whether it's about individuals or groups of people.
Fortunately, trauma isn't the invisible issue it once was. It's all over the nightly news now. Who hasn't seen footage of refugees escaping Syria, for example? It's pretty clear that we're dealing with increasing numbers of traumatized people, and you'd have to go back in a time machine to find any so-called expert who would be skeptical about the legitimacy and impact of trauma. The science is more than abundant, and the damaging effects of trauma on the brain—including across different cultures—is standard knowledge these days.

You know that firsthand because you've seen the ravages of trauma across populations that are very different socioeconomically, culturally, regionally, and so on. It might manifest differently, but trauma affects all of our brains pretty much the same.
Specifically, the brains of mammals have predictable responses to trauma. You can view it through a psychological lens and say, for example, that a dog who's been abused will display very different behavior from a dog who hasn't been traumatized, but trauma's negative impact shows up no matter how you look at it. We mammals have enough neural plasticity to adapt, but having to live in an environment marked with violence and trauma results in a significant negative outcome most of the time.

We're resilient, especially with the right support. And it's important to outline what that entails and make sure trauma survivors have the access they need. At the same time, I don't think people place enough emphasis upon stopping trauma from happening in the first place, especially when you consider that trauma affects the brain in negative ways, which

means more hypervigilance, greater baseline anxiety, avoidance behaviors, and so on.

Post-traumatic resilience and post-traumatic growth are brilliant topics, but I don't think anybody who suffers from trauma is glad it happened. People carry trauma in difficult ways, no matter how they go on to deal with it later.

What we make of something bad that happened to us doesn't negate that the bad thing happened.

That's right. I know refugees who were able to get to the United States, immigrate, learn English, even earn master's degrees in psychology and help lots of people, but at the same time, they still suffer from panic attacks and nightmares about what happened to them. They aren't the same people as they were before the trauma. It's wonderful how they've grown and survived, and in some cases even thrived, but that doesn't change the fact that trauma is fundamentally damaging to human psychology.

That also shows up in how people adapt to traumatic environments. Take the Cambodian genocide, for example. A lot of people who survived—who became most adapted to that horribly traumatic environment—were able to consistently remain so hypervigilant. Situations like that can be terrible and go on for a long time, but they don't tend to be incessant—even World War II and the Holocaust came to an end. And then even the most resilient people in those environments carry that trauma forward.

They looked at a group of survivors of the Cambodian genocide thirty years later—a sample of them living in Massachusetts now—and somewhere between 50 and 70 percent of them screened positive for PTSD. That's a mind-boggling number. What happens on the larger scale with that level of prevalence? Even rates above 20 percent don't make sense to American psychiatrists—it's just not something we've seen.

I don't even know what to do with that data.

Knowing what we do now about epigenetics—how a person's environment changes how their genes function and get passed on—that means lots of different genes are getting activated and deactivated, individually and on a widespread, cultural level. Within family systems, certain traits are being substantially changed as the result of trauma. The children of Holocaust survivors have a much, much higher prevalence of depression, anxiety, and the other kinds of mental health problems that you and I treat. Not surprising at all, because it's basic to the science we now understand. Researchers used to think that it just had to do with parenting, but now we know something about the biological mechanism also.

We're talking about an entire cohort of people who didn't go through the Holocaust, but their brains are still changed by it. Maybe not every single one of them, but enough of them to show up as a pattern in the larger population.

And we're seeing the same thing happen today with what's going on in Syria and the Democratic Republic of the Congo and elsewhere. We can quantify the effects of mass trauma with our knowledge of biological science now as opposed to just talking about it in psychological terms. All of these things are completely intertwined, but the hard science is a bit more convincing. In the last twenty-five years, we've understood the biological and physiological aspects so much better, and there's just no real debate or discussion about whether or not it's a fact at this point.

It's a shame that we have to legitimize what we see right in front of us, but that's the way the world works, and people need hard data. Talking about genes being turned off and connecting that to children behaving differently is the type of evidence that convinces people to take trauma seriously. It makes it harder to turn away from.

That's a lot of the work we do with the courts. Not only can we quantify the brain changes we're talking about but also we can quantify human suffering. That makes a big difference when we're talking about conversations with the United Nations and investigations into human rights violations. The Nuremberg courts after World War II were military tribunals entirely focused on the crimes committed by the Nazis—that's why the attention was on the murders as opposed to the psychological suffering of millions of people who weren't murdered or who somehow endured the Holocaust but suffered immensely.

Those people's lives are changed forever as well as those of their descendants. Violence like that isn't something that plays out within a discrete period of time—the legacy of that violence extends into the future in ways nearly impossible to track.

The Nuremberg trials happened seventy-five years ago, but the same thing occurred regarding rape survivors after Bosnia in the 1990s, which wasn't that long ago. They gathered all of these testimonies from victims in order to prosecute their assailants for rape—the court was interested in the felony, not the aftereffects. They didn't say, "We're also sorry for all you went through. This person is not just responsible for that felony against you but also for the psychology you now manifest, and as reparation, you're entitled to trauma treatment." The shift we're now seeing is starting to consider that. These international tribunals are starting to focus on the effects of trauma that you and I care about—not just the crime but the psychological suffering that results from the crime. That's essential. In addition to nightmares and ongoing anxiety, these rape survivors have been divorced, ostracized from their families, infected with HIV, forced to carry unwanted pregnancies, you name it.

The crime is just the beginning of the story. And that's obviously true when it comes to what's going on in Syria and what happened in Bosnia and World War II and so on, but it's also true regarding traumatic environments that aren't quite at that level. What's happening with the current pandemic, for example—the toll of it will move forward with us.

It's just a matter of time before we see the consequences of Covid-19 coming around in clinical situations and in folks who don't choose to seek help. I've already seen it with some of the community clinics I'm involved with. Domestic violence during the lockdowns has been on the rise, but the story has dropped out of the news, whereas we have women calling the clinics all the time telling us that they're getting beaten, that they're stuck in the house with abusive husbands, that they're having nightmares, and worse. The media have missed the bigger picture, and just focusing on the crime itself is irresponsible reporting in the first place. It's about what's happening downstream, and it's about actually doing something to get these women the help they need.

And the kids involved. And the children who are going to be born in a couple of years. People who haven't been conceived yet will suffer from these problems because these problems are in their parents.

Unbelievable, right? But it's science now. It isn't a theory. And that level of pervasive damage is what some of the UN courts are looking into. Some of these crimes are committed with that degree of trauma in mind, in which the motive is actually to change the psychology of a group of people. I don't want to get overly graphic, but when a military group attacks a village in Iraq and gang rapes the women of that village, it's not about sexual gratification—it's about destroying the psychology of that village. As far as war crimes go, that intent doesn't get enough attention. And when we're looking at the resultant trauma, there's a substantive difference between surviving a tsunami and having an interpersonal crime directed against you. The more personal the trauma, the worse the suffering.

Interpersonally perpetrated. The intent being psychological change over time.

That's right. That's what regimes use as a weapon. My grandfather lived during the Nazi occupation of Holland, and he described what happened whenever anybody tried to escape the work camp—the Nazis would cut their bodies into pieces and then hang the pieces from the trees. What's the intent of that crime? It's certainly not just to punish the person who tried to escape. It's to pummel the rest of the people into submission. When people with power do this, it's called an oppressive tactic as opposed to terrorism, which is when the marginalized group lashes out. Hijacking a plane and flying it into a building is a terrorist act, but terrorists have used oppressive tactics elsewhere. My point here isn't just to talk about horrible, graphic things but to highlight the importance of motive. These criminals understand well that they're going to affect the psychology of the victims, and that's really what they're going for.

A lot of the trauma we experience as a society actually has that psychological intention to it.

Exactly. Institutionalized police brutality is just one example. That's why if you and I (two white men) are driving around, and we get pulled over by the police, we're worried about getting a ticket. Whereas two men of color could be worried about getting killed. And that's not unreasonable. They could interact with the police in the same way that we would and still get shot. Their fear would be justified, and that fear is the result of a legacy of terrible actions by people in power that have happened in real time. It's the same thing with sexual violence and misogyny in our culture. There are terrible traumas that are obvious like rape, but there are microaggressions and microtraumas happening all the time that push a culture in a way that favors the oppressors and damages the oppressed.

It's almost a given in our society that some people have fewer rights than others and some people are more at risk—almost like, "That's just the way it is." That's a hard attitude to counter because we don't typically question it, and it has so much inertia. But questioning those beliefs and the systems built on those beliefs is necessary to alleviate social stratification or at least not perpetuate it. And as you're pointing out, part of the power of oppressive systems is to alter the psychology of a population because trauma results in altered perceptions of the world as well as our place in it. Victor Frankl's writings on Holocaust survivors address that. It's not just PTSD, it's people losing their faith in God because of unimaginable trauma. That's not a diagnosis. That's not in the DSM (*Diagnostic and Statistical Manual of Mental Disorders*). But losing your faith is a monumental change in how you live your life.

And imagine how that cascades out—think about how many perceptions and beliefs and behaviors come with religion. What happens to a person when that falls away?
People who would never think about suicide as an option before the trauma are one example. You have these accounts from Doctors Without Borders and the International Red Cross of religious Syrian refugee mothers leaving their children and killing themselves at sea. That's a complete reversal of worldview. In their culture and religion, these women would never do something like that, but the trauma is so damaging that it changes everything. These are extreme examples I'm talking about, but the same thing happens when the traumatic event isn't as severe. Just a few hits are enough to change the course of someone's reality.

Right. It doesn't take rape or an assault of some other type to change the way you think about the world and yourself. I'm even aware of this in my own life, and I often don't register the traumas I've experienced as that big of a deal. I catch myself sometimes—a new way of thinking about something or somebody I didn't have before my brother and mother died, for example—and that's just what I notice. How many times does that happen without me realizing it? And those weren't even things inflicted upon me personally. Like you said, that aspect of someone harming someone else on purpose makes a big difference.

Sure. Some of the survivors of the Indian Ocean tsunami in 2004 were angry with God, and some weren't, and that has everything to do with how they interpreted the event—how personally they took it. It's the same thing with Cambodia. If your worldview entails the belief in karma, you might ascribe a whole different meaning to being raped and tortured. There are all of these factors that affect resilience and dysfunction. Kids who lost their parents in the tsunami, for example, are clearly suffering—they lost everything important to them, and they're orphans now, and I certainly don't want to diminish the psychiatric outcomes of that. But their worldview matters because worldview is one of the factors that determine how people experience their trauma and how they go on to develop after it happens.

I'm thinking back to people who suffer from personalized trauma— trauma that leaves them feeling singled out and personally attacked—and how utterly damaging that is to the way they experience the world. I think the psychiatric world has missed the boat on that. Like, if it doesn't check the boxes for PTSD, it somehow doesn't matter—it's not actually trauma. I think that's done a huge disservice to people. When people get traumatized, all sorts of syndromic stuff can happen, and one of those things can be PTSD, but there's so much else. Like you said, there's nothing in the *DSM* that accounts for people losing their faith in God.

The PTSD diagnosis is often useful in getting people the help they need, especially when it comes to these international, large-scale traumas we're talking about. Our brains change in predictable ways after trauma, and the *DSM* has captured what the resulting thoughts and behaviors often look like. But PTSD certainly isn't the last word. It's not even a good litmus test. To your point, there have been some asylum cases in which a survivor doesn't check the boxes for PTSD, so the case gets reconsidered, and incorrect assumptions are made. An incorrect assumption like if the asylum seeker doesn't have PTSD, their trauma isn't important. That's an entirely backward process and way of thinking about trauma.

PTSD is an excellent indicator that you are suffering problematically from trauma, but you can be suffering from some pretty damaging trauma and not have PTSD. PTSD is relevant and useful as a diagnosis, but it's just

looking at a subset of trauma, and the idea that only "real trauma" manifests as PTSD is truly problematic. I see this individually with patients who suffer from trauma that might not be the same caliber as the terrible things that happen to people in a war zone, but that are still life changing. And because they don't check the boxes for PTSD, their suffering somehow doesn't count. Worse, sometimes they're even told they're faking it. Like, "You don't have PTSD, so it isn't real." Either that or "Your traumatic experience wasn't all that bad."

Exactly.
That's terrible.

People with trauma get invalidated all the time. People have discernible and consistent problems that clearly come as the result of trauma, but they're ignored or dismissed because it doesn't line up with the PTSD diagnosis.
We're taking that into account now with our reports to the international courts. PTSD is still a part of the picture, but we're also informing them of the other manifestations of trauma—measurable things that lead to dysfunction. That's important when it comes to these sophisticated situations with international prosecutors and defense attorneys and judges. By and large, these judges are very intellectual and receptive, and they appreciate having the facts laid out for them.

One of the aims of this book is to show that trauma and PTSD aren't the same thing, and it's validating to know you're doing similar work on the international scale. Clearly trauma happens when a person is raped or in combat, but in those situations, the range of possible outcomes includes more than just PTSD. Also, trauma happens in far more situations than rape or combat. That's what I'm trying to say here—to really get the word out about just how prevalent and misunderstood and important trauma is.
You'd think that would be common sense by now. Shakespeare wrote about it, we've had countless studies on trauma by now . . . it's even in the recent remake of Disney's *Beauty and the Beast*, where they show how the Beast became who he was because of childhood trauma. We were recently involved in a case with the Center for Constitutional Rights, and

they were looking into solitary confinement as a violation of the Eighth Amendment—cruel and unusual punishment. The case used a definition for long-term solitary confinement as ten years or longer. Not ten days, but ten years. And we were consulted to examine whether or not we'd find psychiatric changes in men who'd been confined alone in a tiny cell for that long. We interviewed one guy who'd been in solitary for twenty-five years for a crime he'd committed when he was a teenager. Does anybody actually think that man is going to resemble somebody who hasn't been in solitary confinement for twenty-five years? Do you really need a professor of psychiatry to weigh in on that? It is common sense. The proof about trauma has been out there forever—we just need to pay attention as the vast science continues to build.

CHAPTER 8

Social Ills, Social Trauma

When the iron curtain finally fell in the early 1990s, I ventured to places I'd never dreamed of visiting just months earlier. I crossed into Hungary on foot and later spent time in the former Czechoslovakia. In both countries, people were excited to meet an American, and I was equally excited to meet them. I remember my time with them as suffused with the spirit of hope, and I felt aligned with my country's principles of truth, human rights, fairness, and equal opportunity for everyone to strive for a better life.

That was thirty years ago. How did we get so far off course?

The answer to that question is complicated, and it depends on who you ask. I don't think now's the time to argue—as long as trauma is tearing us apart, we should be more concerned with working together to right the ship.

During the cold war, I experienced a United States in which citizens were largely convinced their country was a force of good. We weren't perfect—far from it—but overall, we oriented ourselves toward freedom and civility. We might have debated how best to do that, but when we did so we weren't as vicious and insulting as we are today. We knew we had much in common, and politicians on both sides of the aisle generally behaved with some decorum, and we certainly expected them to. After all, we were Americans, and we needed to save our energy and resources for the common enemy.

The middle school I attended was run with pretty tight discipline. That being said, kids are kids, and one day us kids decided to have an all-out food fight in the lunchroom, basically turning the place into a garbage dump. The school punished us by making us march up and down the hallways after we cleaned it all up, and I can remember reflecting on how stupid we'd all been. We were just a bunch of kids from the same town, and we were always hungry at lunch. Even so, instead of eating our food, we'd thrown it at each another, and now we had to stomp around like soldiers for the rest of the day.

The situation in our country right now is certainly more serious than a food fight, but somehow the lesson still holds. We're all just a bunch of people from the same country, and we're all hungry for something—a sense of safety, a return to stability, reliable nourishment (literal and figurative). And the consequences of our behavior are fairly dire because we're hurling aggression and traumatizing each other. We've become our own (worst) common enemy.

The Boy in the Gas Mask

I was able to visit the Soviet Union in 1990, when the rules had changed enough to allow for supervised tourism to places tourists never went before. These rules weren't always as clear to the local people, however. I was part of a group that toured an elementary school in a town that hadn't seen outsiders since the end of World War II, and the Russian children were told just before we arrived that a group of Americans was coming. I was the first in my assigned group to enter the classroom, and the first thing I saw was a terrified young boy. He was about ten years old. He was wearing a fifty-year-old gas mask.

He didn't run away when I came in, or hide behind the teacher, or put up his fists to fight. In the chaos of the frightening information he and his peers had received that Americans were coming, the boy simply put on his gas mask and waited for whatever awful thing was coming next. All of the kids had been given out-of-date masks like these; there were bridges and buildings in the town that still hadn't been repaired since World War II.

I asked a lot of questions, and one of the supervising guides stepped out of her formal role, and we had a real conversation. She herself had been one of these children once. They were all taught that war was always just around the corner and that the next people to come for them were going to be Americans.

Think about what it's like to grow up in that kind of environment, fearing violence from outsiders constantly. This boy didn't understand global politics or how the world was changing—he simply knew there was a menace just waiting to destroy him. How could he possibly have felt safe or secure? How could any child in that situation feel safe or secure?

❧REFLECTION   If you grew up during the cold war in the United States, what's your side of this experience? How safe and secure did you feel during that time of your life? How might the larger social traumas of the cold war be playing out for adults in the United States today?

THREE CRISES

Among the various issues facing the United States today, I want to highlight three that I see having ongoing impacts for Americans when it comes to trauma: the Covid-19 pandemic, systemic racism and racial injustice, and the erosion of our socioeconomic foundation. For anyone reading this, I probably don't have to say much about the impacts of the first issue. To date, hundreds of thousands of Americans have died from the virus, not to mention how it's affected nearly every aspect of public life imaginable for everyone else, including those grieving their loved ones. Racism is a different issue entirely because Americans have such varied responses to it. Even so, there's no doubting that racism and the conversation about racism are at the forefront of our nation.

In conjunction with other issues, the virus and racial injustice have eroded our confidence in the reliability and promise of our socioeconomic foundation. That foundation is the bedrock of our nation, holding up our values of hope and dignity. That being said, entire essential industries—the farming and service industries, for example—have just gotten by over the past few decades, and the dream of getting ahead by devoting one's life to careers in them has almost become a pipe dream. Mounting debt, job insecurity, and the loss of basic housing for millions of Americans has brought us to a precarious point, and a nation full of people just struggling to survive isn't one that can devote itself to compassion, community, and humanity.

Nowhere do we see this more clearly expressed than in prejudice that results in violence and death. To make matters even more difficult, those of us insulated by privilege have trouble relating to the traumas inflicted upon our kindred citizens, far too many of them living with constant fear and anxiety. It's our responsibility, then, to do what we can to help, to speak out, and to refuse to turn away from racism and prejudice whenever and wherever we encounter it. We can do this by demanding change to our systems permeated with racism, by condemning the violence and lost opportunities racism generates, and by simply acknowledging that all of us share the same rights and should be able to count on those rights being respected by others.

Am I Doing a Bad Job?

As I discussed a couple of chapters ago, the medical field has become one of the worst offenders at prioritizing rules and guidelines over people's needs. Earlier in my career, I took over care for a group of patients with high levels of mental illness—people in the system for a long time who almost never got any better. In trying to help one of them, I apparently did a bad job while believing I was doing a good one.

One patient in the group was a large, middle-aged man who always wore a thick trench coat. He was stern and intimidating, and everyone seemed to be afraid of him except the receptionists because they were used to him and knew that he had no known history of violence. This man was required to come to psychiatry appointments by a social services order, but he never actually went into the doctor's office because he suspected that everyone wanted to harm him. He wouldn't even let people walk behind him.

Because of his fear, the man's appointments were limited to visiting the waiting room, where he would exchange a few words with the doctor to clarify that he would not cooperate. Over time, I built a rapport with him by visiting with him in the corner of the waiting room, and eventually he trusted me enough to walk to my office (but not go inside), with me walking in front of him. So, we had brief sessions at the doorway of my office, and that's where I learned more about his history than was included in the files.

This man had suffered a lot from racism in his life. We were able to talk about that directly, and over time he was able to trust me a little more. I also found out that he truly did want help. He heard voices all of the time, his brain had trouble grasping time commitments, he had trouble tracking when he was hungry or tired, and his family was severely impoverished. The only way he was able to make it to my office on time was because his wife put him on the right bus to the clinic each week. Probably the most difficult thing for him was that he was unable to be a good father to his ten-year-old son. They loved each other, but my patient was simply too sick. More than anything, he wanted to go to his son's baseball games, cheer him on, and show the boy how proud he was.

The more trust we built, the more open he was to taking the medicine he needed, and the more he came into the actual room of my office. After the medicine started working, he became less paranoid, the voices didn't bother him as much, and his thoughts became more organized. He was able to spend more time with his son. He was even able to fulfill his wish of attending the boy's baseball games. One of the most rewarding calls I've received came from his tearful wife, who described how angry she'd been at the system before, how her husband had never before received the help he actually needed, and how grateful she was that he was now taking his medicine and learning how to father his son.

Later, I received a notice that I'd been flagged for substandard work. I'd been documenting partial visits in the waiting room and all of that time he spent in my doorway, and that was a big no-no. Apparently, if he didn't want to come into the office, I was supposed to let him leave, and I was also accused of reinforcing his paranoia by allowing him to always walk behind me. The help my patient needed did not fit the requirements of a system he had every right to mistrust. Because of their race and poverty, both he and his wife had come to expect no assistance whatsoever, and the system wasn't actually designed to pay them much attention anyway.

REFLECTION Our social systems are supposed to be there for the benefit of all of us. Sadly, that's often not the case. What additional traumas did this man and his family needlessly experience because of the rules and requirements of an insensitive system? Think of a time when you or someone you love was ignored, dismissed, or outright denied by an agency or organization expected to help. What was that like? How does it compare with this man's experience?

TRAUMA AND THE ASSAULT ON COMPASSION, COMMUNITY, AND HUMANITY

The problems and solutions we see in front of us depend on the lenses through which we view the world. This is just as true for me as it is for anyone, and—as I repeat often in this book—trauma has an insidious way of altering our lenses. Ideally, we can become more curious about these lenses and the ways in which our experiences, beliefs, and the ideas of others come to color our world.

When I reflect on my own life, I'm struck with the feeling that there have been two distinct parts—the part before the major traumas in my life occurred and the part that followed. Beforehand, the world made more sense to me, and I felt confident in my ability to understand it—at least enough not to feel vulnerable all the time. My experience is quite different in the second part of my life. More often than not, I feel alarmed about what's happening in the world, and I don't have the same confidence in my own understanding or ability to navigate whatever's coming my way. In part, this change in my lens has to do with my own individual traumas, but it isn't just that. There are larger trends afoot that change how all of us view the world.

As members of a society, it's beyond our power to totally eliminate trauma. Our parents die, car accidents happen, and illness is a biological fact. That being said, we can do a much better job at preventing unnecessary traumas from killing us and even from taking hold of us in the first place. A bitterly divisive social environment is the nemesis of trauma prevention. The political climate we now find ourselves in has somehow allowed personal insults and assaults to become acceptable, if not the norm. Far too many of us have become allergic to people who differ from us and have developed the tendency to turn away from those who don't resemble us, regardless of the degree of their suffering. The social erosion of compassion, community, and humanity has paved the way for more trauma that weakens the very foundation of our country. This damage is amplified as too many people drape themselves in a flag that's supposed to stand for all of us.

> Trauma pushes us to take steps away from life and away from each other.

There are powerful forces that divide us, but I believe the forces that unite us are even stronger. I say this as someone who's worked in medicine for more than twenty years in a variety of settings—ERs, nursing homes, inner-city hospitals, and community clinics—and with people of all races and religions who span the continuum from homelessness to enormous wealth. I can tell you as a fact that trauma affects us all. Some of us have definitely suffered more hits than others, but trauma does remarkably similar (and predictable) things to people no matter who we are. In a strange way, trauma is what divides us, but it's also what unites us all.

Like trauma itself, societal conflict is mostly inevitable. However, when we become more interested in generating and propagating conflict than we are in resolving it in a just way, that conflict serves as fuel for more harm and risk—especially for those already at risk—and that creates even more trauma. It's a vicious loop that feels like it's becoming more dangerous by the day. We're familiar with these types of self-propagating loops in family dynamics, at work, and within friendships, but trauma cycles on the societal level make everything worse for all of us.

Trauma and shame and society's neglect promote sickness and dysfunction and violence. They also shape our dialogue as a society and prevent us from solving the very problems they cause. Trauma pushes us to take steps away from life and away from each other. Trauma pushes us toward fear and vulnerability, and it creates false signposts that guide us toward the murky depths of isolation and suffering. If we're not careful and if we don't stand together, we can lose ourselves in a maze of shame, repeating unhealthy choices, sabotaging our own well-being, and causing harm to others—others suffering from trauma just as we are.

We haven't decided to abandon our civic dialogue and turn our backs on the fundamental values of our democracy, but they are under attack nonetheless. The pervasiveness of social media in our lives has enabled us to remain at home by ourselves and rarely interact with others, while finding validation for virtually any point of view imaginable in an arena in which the strongest, most outrageous, and often most aggressive opinions leave the greatest footprint. And the more worked up we get, the less curious we become about other points of view, especially those belonging to people who don't look like us, think like us, or visit the same news sites and chatrooms. Instead of diversity being synonymous with richness, it's increasingly viewed with suspicion and animosity.

Why are so many of us so irritated and frustrated, like boiling kettles with no outlet for the steam, rumbling menacingly and threatening to explode? I look around me (and in the mirror), and I see how trauma, shame, and all the other accomplices force this way of being upon us. Trauma makes us alienated from ourselves, angry and outraged with ourselves, without the ability to live with ourselves. And if we can't live with ourselves, how can we live with other people? Trauma fogs the mirror and distorts the window. We then can't see ourselves as we are, and we can't view the differences of others as anything other than harmful. This needs to change.

CHAPTER 9

Social Ills, Social Solutions

arger problems call for larger, all-encompassing solutions. Although this book mostly focuses on the individual experience of trauma and how to prevent trauma and alleviate its symptoms on that level, the societal factors discussed in part II of this book clearly call for some helpful suggestions. What I offer here isn't exhaustive, but I hope you'll find something in this chapter that helps you gain a foothold when it comes to socially generated (and socially experienced) traumas.

ANTIDOTE: *Fostering Humility*

It surprises and frightens me to see leaders proven unquestionably wrong double down on their mistakes and avoid taking responsibility for their actions at any cost. The popularity of this strategy creates an environment that prioritizes self-interest and favors bullying over civility. What's with the growing lack of humility in the world?

Humility allows us to learn from our interactions and enables us to compromise. Humility empowers us to recognize the humanity of people who don't look like us or who hold beliefs we find unusual and foreign. Humility, too, reminds us that burning bridges hurts all of us. Considering all that, you'd think our leaders would do a better job of modeling humility for us.

The reason they often don't has to do with the way we confuse humility with shame. And that crucial mistake comes down to trauma. Because we're infected with trauma, we experience shame and often anger as well. When a situation calls for us to contact and express natural humility, we then see it through the lens of anger or shame. If anger, we look upon others with arrogance and aggression; if shame, we look away. Sometimes that looking away is more like frantic flailing to avoid something dreaded—as if a person were drowning and lost in panic. But the flailing becomes indistinguishable from aggression, and both hurt anyone who happens to be nearby. In this way, our pain—regardless of which form it takes—becomes weaponized. Weaponized pain tends to hurt others, and that hurt often takes the form of shaming. Sometimes the weapons are more severe—separating parents from their children, for example, and putting the children in cages. Regardless of what the weapons look like, trauma wins out. The more misery there is in the world, the more shame and anger, and the whole cycle keeps going around and around, picking up steam as it goes.

We can't fix our fundamental problems until we face up to this and hold ourselves and others accountable. What would it be like to be more oriented to compromise than to being right? How can we demand our leaders in government, business, religion, and so on take a stance against the trauma cycle and prioritize humility and civility? These solutions are readily within reach, but, like most things we want to change in life, we often have to begin with ourselves.

ANTIDOTE: *Remembering Our Core Values*

Imagine one group of people who lived together for thousands and thousands of years. A few generations back, the group split into two tribes who now see themselves as enemies with nothing in common. Because they live in different places now, one tribe worships the river god; the other worships the sun god. Whenever there's a drought, the river god people kidnap some of the sun god worshippers and drown them. Whenever there's a flood, the sun god people kidnap some of the river god worshippers and burn them at the stake. Despite these sacrifices, droughts and floods keep happening. In fact, it seems to be getting worse. That's because there's no god in persecution—no river god, no sun god. There aren't any values or solutions in persecution. There's only suffering, and suffering begets more suffering.

This isn't a critique of religion. In my opinion, most of the core values of the world's religions are worth following, especially those that emphasize compassion, community, and humanity. Religious values themselves aren't the problem; the problem comes when we twist these values beyond all recognition. Trauma causes us to do this because it distorts our values and weaponizes them against others—especially those who are different and especially those who are vulnerable.

Persecution is antithetical to compassion, community, and humanity, and we must become aware of all the ways—blatant and subtle—that persecution manifests. Whether it's denying consenting adults the right to marry, keeping work hours just below the benefits threshold, abusing power as a public official, or punishing people fleeing the ravages of their own country to seek refuge in ours, acts of social persecution destroy the compassion, community, and humanity our world should stand for. Only trauma, its accomplices, and the suffering they generate could twist beyond recognition the values of truth and dignity that are our birthright and are supposedly the foundation of any country calling itself a democracy. We are better than this; we can do better than this.

Cancer and car accidents and earthquakes and viruses create more than enough trauma to go around. If we keep making more trauma, it might just be the end of us. Fortunately, we still have a choice in the matter. All it takes is enough of us saying, "Enough is enough!" and remembering our core values as citizens of the same planet. It's a general antidote, but one you can personalize for yourself. If you believe in compassion, community, and humanity, please find a way to place those values in the forefront of your life, for the benefit of us all.

The Murder That Was and the Assault That Wasn't

When I was traveling along the border between Thailand and Myanmar twenty-five years ago, I spent time at a guesthouse that had a varied clientele. Travelers from everywhere passed through there—refugees from China and Laos, adventurers in search of treasure, drug runners, and a few missionaries. One night while I was there, one of the long-term residents pushed another long-term resident off of a high cliff above the river that separates the two countries. The attacker was discovered later stealing money out of the room of the person he'd pushed off the cliff.

When the owner of the guesthouse found out, he rushed out to find the victim. It was possible to survive the fall from the cliff, he said, but the river would sweep the person downstream, and he'd need help. I found myself on the back of the owner's motorcycle, speeding off downstream to see what we could do.

After we arrived and got off the bike, we were searching the riverbanks for only a few minutes when the guesthouse owner tackled me with enough force to knock the wind out of me. I lay there in the mud trying to catch my breath, and when I looked over, there next to me was the owner as well. He gestured for me to be silent and to stay absolutely still, and then he whispered something I probably should have learned before we set out—I'd been shining my flashlight on the opposite bank of the river, and that had been enough in the past for the Myanmar sentries to shoot to kill. That's why he'd tackled me—to save my life.

We never found the victim. After returning to the United States, I learned that he'd died—his body was found farther downstream. His death was the result of cold inhumanity, but my surviving that night might have been the result of the owner's willingness to risk his life for my own. I never found out any more about the murderer, but I imagine his trauma history is a mile long. And so is the cascade of trauma that followed his action—the physical and mental pain of the man he pushed off the cliff, the loss that followed for his fiancée (she was a refugee and dependent on his support), the grief and confusion of the victim's family, and on and on. Trauma comes from trauma; trauma begets trauma.

REFLECTION Has anyone ever risked their life to save yours? Have you put yourself in harm's way to protect others? Would you do so again? Who would you sacrifice yourself for? Who not?

ANTIDOTE: *Opening Ourselves to Others*

The more vulnerable people are, the more difficult their recovery from trauma can be. People whom society disenfranchises or discriminates against encounter additional obstacles when asking for or receiving help in a world where prejudice is abundant and competent assistance is in short supply. Those of us with privilege can help others who have less, especially those suffering from racism. One step in doing this is to do your best to understand that their lived experience differs substantially from your own, open yourself up to their pervasive sense of vulnerability, and feel it as if it were your own.

I recently watched a news clip of a black man expressing his despair and harrowing fears for the safety of his son. He was having trouble sleeping because he kept worrying that his son might get shot simply because of the color of his skin. It's easy to turn away from the suffering of others, especially when you're watching it on your computer or television, and even more so when you don't identify with the person. In this case, I'm white, I don't have a son, and I'm not worried that my child might be killed because of racism. In one sense, I'm nothing like that man. But if I can access our shared humanness and do my best to open myself up to his experience, that's one step toward increasing the compassion, community, and humanity in the world, and reducing the ravages of trauma.

ANTIDOTE: *Managing Fear*

When there seems to be so much bad news in the world, it's critical that we allow ourselves to feel it without remaining in a constant state of fear. This is more than an individual issue because our nervous systems affect those of others, which is helpful to remember when it comes to our children, spouses, parents, friends, and community members. We all have our thresholds, and after a certain point too much anxiety causes deleterious effects. At the time I'm writing this, the world is still struggling with the Covid-19 pandemic—millions of people have been infected, and hundreds of thousands in the United States alone have died from the virus (nearly one quarter of the world's deaths are in the United States). The anxiety the virus has generated has spread even faster than the illness itself, and the additional problems created by fear bring even more stress to an already traumatized society. Here are a few ideas for taking the heat off that fear and managing it as best you can:

- **MAINTAIN HEALTHY ROUTINES OR MAKE NEW ONES.** Practice self-care by getting enough sleep, exercising, and eating a healthy diet.

- **REDUCE EXPOSURE.** It's easy to stoke the fires of fear; it's a lot harder to put them out when they're raging. Know your limits when it comes to media exposure, stressful conversations, and negative thought patterns.

- **FOCUS ON WHAT'S IMPORTANT.** Reflect on what matters most to you, and let other things go. Take stock of your values and what behaviors are in line with those values. Do what you can to spend as much time in a given day aligned with what's most important to you.

- **ASK FOR HELP.** None of us are meant to do it all by ourselves. Compassion, community, and humanity also mean reaching out to others and allowing them to help you. When fear begins to take its toll, be sure to reach out to family members, friends, and any mental health care services or other organizations in your community that you trust.

ANTIDOTE: *Avoiding Quick Fixes*

Most of us are accustomed to answers at our fingertips—when a problem presents itself, we expect a straightforward solution. In chapter 6, I talked about the damaging results of this trend in health care, but the truth is most of us are far too susceptible to relying on short-term solutions to complex problems. In the end, the solutions don't work, and we're left with more difficulties than we began with.

We get hungry and grab the closest/cheapest junk food. Our hunger goes away for a little bit, but the ongoing habit makes obesity, heart disease, and diabetes more likely. We watch with horror as the media show us yet another story of children murdering their peers at school, and we devolve into debates about gun rights that do nothing to ensure the future safety of our children. We spend money before we've actually earned it, spiraling into further debt that ensures we'll never earn enough to break even. We encounter people with different opinions and approaches to life than ours, but instead of reaching out to them with interest and curiosity, we shut them out, insult or demean them, and in some cases deny their basic rights. We take the clickbait and purchase things we never intended to buy, or read the same distressing news story over and over again in different packages.

It's helpful at times to take an inventory of our actions and readjust accordingly. Whatever stressor you're facing, do your best to analyze whether the options you're considering are actually going to solve the issue down the road. Caring for ourselves and others—as well as caring for the world—require us to reexamine our actions and beliefs from time to time. Doing so will help alleviate the trauma we share and stop more trauma from occurring in the future.

PART THREE

AN OWNER'S MANUAL
FOR YOUR BRAIN

———

A billion stars go spinning through the night,
blazing high above your head.
But in you is the presence that
will be, when all the stars are dead.

RAINER MARIA RILKE, "BUDDHA IN GLORY"

CHAPTER 10

What Trauma Does to Thought

When I was in my mid-thirties, I had completed five years of college across four institutions in two countries, and I'd also graduated from medical school and completed hospital rotations in psychiatry and neurology. It took all of that experience for me to realize I was just then learning a set of lessons I should have learned in middle school.

A description of that set of lessons would look a lot like the contents of this book. It would include the importance of affect, feeling, and emotion (more on them in chapter 11) as well as how these three can overrule logic, change our memories, and even alter what those memories mean. It would include an explanation of how contagious trauma is as well as its role as an invisible conductor of a vast orchestra of unhappiness. The lessons would also reveal how shame and its accomplices hijack our brains and elucidate how trauma paves the way for depression, addiction, fear-driven isolation, and cycles of violence that expand from home to community to nation to world. These are just a few of the things I believe children should learn at an early age—in an age-appropriate way, of course. I'd call it "An Owner's Manual for Your Brain."

LOGIC, EMOTION, AND MEMORY

We like to think of ourselves as mostly logical creatures, but the truth is we have complex systems in our brains both for logic and for emotion. The input from these systems has to be integrated by the brain for us to make decisions, and if the systems are saying the same thing, it's fairly easy to make decisions. This would be like two people who get to choose one (and only one) flavor of ice cream to share—if they both want the same flavor, no problem. But what if they disagree? This is where things get interesting.

Ultimately, emotion is more deeply rooted in the brain than logic because our more emotional aspects are evolutionarily older. That means in important matters, if our brain is tallying two votes—one for logic and one for emotion—it defaults to however emotion votes. For example, if someone we love is trapped in a burning building, logic tells us that going in is a bad idea, whereas emotion tells us to rush in headlong. That's why we've all heard stories of people risking their lives for others even when the odds were against them.

Of course, the brain is more nuanced than simple all-or-nothing decision making. If possible, it will do what it can to integrate both logic and emotion. To continue the ice cream scenario, if logic wants chocolate and emotion wants vanilla, the person might very well leave the ice cream shop with a scoop of each (or a small scoop of chocolate and a big scoop of vanilla so that emotion can have the upper hand). If there's no clear compromise to be had, the brain might allow logic to think it's running the show right up until the actual decision is made, but emotion is sneakily having its say the whole time. So, logic wants chocolate and emotion wants vanilla. Logic states its case: We haven't had chocolate in a while, for example, and everybody says this place has the best chocolate ice cream in town. Emotion whispers in the background that chocolate is more fattening and that it often leads to nausea at bedtime, even though these things might not be true. The brain has already sided with logic by this point—its argument was convincing enough—and on the walk to the ice cream shop, the brain starts thinking about other things. Then the person walks up to the counter and, without thinking about it, orders two scoops of vanilla.

Trauma changes our emotions; changed emotions determine our decisions.

What happened? Basically, emotion has been whispering in the background the whole time, pushing whatever vanilla buttons it can find, and the brain is actually listening to what emotion's telling it below the surface of awareness. This is how emotion gets its way, often without us recognizing just how convincing it is or how to wield its power in a helpful way.

This is where shame and trauma's other accomplices come into play without our knowing it because they directly influence our emotions and the emotional aspect of decision making. Our decisions seem based in logic, but our trauma-tinted emotions are actually calling the shots. Maybe we don't apply for that great job because we've become afraid of failure, or maybe we don't ask somebody out (who's clearly available and interested) because our self-confidence is in the dumps, or maybe we stop taking care of ourselves (eating right, exercising, getting enough sleep, etc.) because we don't believe we deserve to feel healthy and good in the world. Trauma changes our emotions; changed emotions determine our decisions.

I had a patient—an extremely smart and personable young woman—who declined a college scholarship to stay put with her boyfriend. The young man drank too much, verbally abused her, and occasionally hit her, convincing her that it was her fault. When we talked about their relationship and her decision to remain with him despite other opportunities, she sounded so calm and logical. Trauma and shame had hijacked her brain to convince her that she'd never find anyone better than him and that she didn't deserve a better life anyway. It was so reasonable to her to decline the scholarship and stay where she was, essentially giving up on any hope of a better relationship and future.

Sadly, there's a lot more to the story. I'd known this young woman for a long time. Earlier in her life, she'd been excited about her potential and all the things she'd go on to achieve in life, and she had a healthy self-image. She liked herself for all the good qualities everyone else enjoyed about her—she was smart, funny, and kind. Then, during her mid-teens, certain factors in her parents' relationship led them to neglect her, and she began to get the message that she wasn't worth their time and attention. They stopped monitoring her whereabouts and activities, and she began to care less about her whereabouts and activities, too. She began taking risks she never would have considered before, and a couple of predatory people from school took advantage of her. After a series of sexual assaults, she viewed herself as damaged; even worse, she was convinced it was her own fault.

This young woman forgot how she'd felt about herself before. The girl who was so hopeful about the future was now plagued with thoughts and emotions that convinced her otherwise. It wasn't just that she didn't think she deserved to be treated well; these new ideas and emotions told her that she didn't deserve *not to be hurt*. The young woman I first knew as a teenager is dead now. She didn't commit suicide—not exactly. But she did stop caring for herself and got hooked on drugs, and that upped the chances dramatically that she'd die "by accident."

I don't hold her responsible for the changes in herself or the abandonment of her self-care. Instead, I hold responsible trauma and a society that looks the other way as it unfolds in predictable patterns, including our tendency to blame victims for their suffering. We get used to the heartless idea that this is just the way it is—that some people are destined to die in this way—but I don't believe it. This woman's death was entirely avoidable. It can't be undone, but I hope to bring some justice to her and to others who have suffered a similar fate. It begins by looking trauma in the face and putting a stop to this terrible madness.

COGNITIVE BLINDERS

Among the most frightening consequences of trauma are the blinders that it secretly constructs in our brains in order to steal from us. Imagine a thief builds a giant wall in front of a house and then paints the wall to look exactly like the front of the house. Passers-by think that it's the same house and that everything is just fine, while the thief is operating behind the façade to steal the actual house. Trauma's the thief, and blinders are the wall it creates in front of what it wants.

We usually think of blinders in the visual sense, but I'm actually using it here to describe how certain knowledge gets walled off in the brain, so much so that we can't even remember what was there in the first place. And we don't typically go looking for things that we don't know exist. This is how we lose the awareness that we're good people, that we deserve to be happy, that we should expect to be treated with kindness, and that we don't have to stand for abuse of any type. In our minds, we think we know just about everything we knew before—that we just keep learning more and more stuff—but that's not how it works with trauma.

Those of us who have suffered from trauma invariably have cognitive blinders of one form or another.

Remember the map I mentioned in chapter 5? We think what we're look-ing at is the same map we were using before, but we have no idea some crucial information has been erased. In fact, the map has been falsified to lure us to where the dragons are, and we haven't the slightest idea it's happened. Life is hard enough to navigate even with the most accurate and helpful maps. Add cognitive blinders to the mix, and our odds start to plummet, mainly because some of the most serious threats to our safety and well-being are those we don't normally see.

I was recently at a train museum with my children, and we saw an exhibit that stressed the importance of making sure to look both ways and to listen at every train crossing—pay extra attention, scan left and right, turn down the radio so that you can hear better, and so on. The overarching lesson was never to cross the tracks until you're completely sure there isn't a train bar-reling down on you, which seemed to me good advice. The consequences of missing out on certain information are fairly dire.

Those of us who have suffered from trauma invariably have cognitive blinders of one form or another. This can make it even more difficult to dodge life's hazards—train-sized or otherwise—so it's up to us to learn how trauma modifies our brains and hides important facets of the world from us (including certain memories). There are a number of ways to do this: reflection (like some of the reflections offered in this book), discussing our experiences and perceptions with others (trusted friends, for example), and seeking professional help when we need it.

It's crucial that we operate with an accurate view of ourselves as well as a clear and wide view of the world around us. We need to free ourselves of con-vincingly painted walls that look like the treasures trauma has stolen from us. We need those treasures. And we need to be free of the threats trauma hurls at us from behind the barriers it erects, threats that tell us we aren't good enough, or that people don't like us, or that we deserve to be hurt, or that it will never work out.

There are countless ways cognitive blinders work to convince us life isn't what we once hoped it would be. Trauma makes us forget, it makes us remember the wrong things, and it steers us down paths we never wanted to embark on in the first place. The key to countering this is learning how to stop new blinders from taking root and unrooting the ones already constructed inside us.

Who Put My Patient on the Train Tracks?

The person on the phone asked me whether I knew who put my patient on the train tracks. I didn't know how to answer the question, and it was being asked with considerable urgency.

I quickly learned that my patient had been found lying between the rails. She had no injury that would indicate being hit on the head, but she was unconscious when she was found. A jogger on a nearby path had seen her, and fearing she was dead, he reached out to touch her. This caused her to sit up in alarm and scream for help. The man called the police and did his best to calm her, but even the police were at a loss when they showed up. While they were waiting for the ambulance to arrive, someone let her use their phone, and my patient called me.

"Who put me on the train tracks?" she asked.

Like I said, I didn't know what to say. It wasn't that I didn't know the answer, and I was fairly certain that she knew the answer, too. It was her. She had put my patient on the train tracks.

She was a shy and kind older woman. She was the kind of person who faded easily into the background anywhere she went, and that wasn't by accident. Hiding—including hiding in broad daylight—had become second nature to her. The woman had been through a lot of trauma in her life, and her tribulations had started early in life. Hiding had become ingrained as a coping strategy essentially since birth. My patient had carved out a peaceful existence for herself, but it was punctuated by terror and flight, sometimes without warning, and occasionally with great danger. Being found unconscious on the train tracks was one such episode.

"Who put me on the train tracks?" she repeated.

I knew it wouldn't work to tell her the truth. We both knew her history, but there was no way she was going to accept my answer. I had been working to help her come to realize that she was one being with one mind, no matter how fragmented it felt at times, and I was making some headway. She worked hard in therapy, and she often evinced tremendous bravery in allowing herself to be so vulnerable. It was a different story entirely when she was triggered, and the triggering—as well as the ensuing terror and flight—were utterly unpredictable. Sometimes the trigger would come from an understandably related event, such as reading a news story about someone being violently attacked; sometimes the trigger seemed innocuous—seeing a child that looked sad, for example. Whenever this happened, her sense of self would shatter into multiple pieces.

There were several other people my patient might become, and all of them were split-off parts of herself. One of them was terribly afraid and would hide in closets and under beds, never leaving the house for anything. Another would eat all of the food in the house. She wasn't particularly worried about these two, but a couple of the others were incredibly resistant to any efforts to integrate. One of them was angry and punitive. It told her abhorrent things, including that she didn't deserve to live. The other came across as extremely protective. It soothed her by saying she'd be a lot safer if only she weren't alive.

This is what she was asking me. She wanted to know which one of these parts of herself put her on the train tracks. She desperately wanted to know, and she wanted to know right then and there. She wanted to know which one to blame for the incident.

I wanted to console her in the moment and talk later about what happened. My idea was that we could explore the triggering event, what it led to, and what we could learn from it to help her in the future. I didn't want her to blame anyone because that would mean taking it out on a part of herself.

"I'm sorry," I said, and I repeated it several times. I said it like I meant it, and I did. She protested that I wasn't answering her question, and I kept telling her I was sorry. I didn't know if it was the right thing to do, but I kept saying I was sorry anyway. After a while she stopped talking and started quietly crying. It was the first time I'd ever felt a genuine connection to her.

Our minds are amazingly complex. We carry within us so many different ways of knowing ourselves and understanding the world around us. When we're healthy, we can knit all of this together into a consistent sense of self, and that self can access a consistent set of behavioral choices to navigate the world. It's hard, but usually we can do it.

Add trauma to the picture, and it changes the whole story. It becomes harder for us to focus, and whatever focus we can muster is filtered over with the lenses of negative affects, feelings, and emotions. As with my patient, trauma in early life can crack the lens and shatter any coherent sense of what it means to be a human being.

REFLECTION　We all have various aspects of ourselves. They might not act like separate personalities, but they often seem to have competing agendas difficult to resolve. What are your pieces? What characters or voices do you encounter in yourself that sometimes make it harder to live the way you'd prefer to live? How might trauma have influenced the way these aspects speak to you?

VICTIMIZATION AND THE VICTIM MINDSET

Unfortunately, far too many of us qualify as victims. I'm speaking in the legal sense, in which one person is attacked or otherwise harmed by another—such people qualify as victimized, and they deserve recourse not only for the crime committed against them but also for the ensuing trauma. Sometimes being victimized is merely a matter of inconvenience (as when someone smashed my car window and stole my favorite Mozart tape) and sometimes it's much, much worse (e.g., the patient I described in chapter 1 who was raped leaving her friend's party). I want to make it clear that this isn't the type of victim or victimization I'm referring to here.

How many of us suffer from a constant narrative of negative self-talk?

Instead, I want to discuss how people can become victims in the psychological sense, as when they conclude that the world is categorically out to get them. Of course, this idea can sometimes result from trauma as a way in which cognitive blinders manifest. We deem the world fundamentally dangerous, and our blinders show us only where that's true. This is where *selective abstraction* comes into play.

Imagine everything about your day has gone well—your children actually listened to you, everyone pulled their weight at work, the traffic on your way home was decent, and your spouse had your favorite meal waiting for you when you walked through the door. Whatever works for you, think of that. Now imagine that something at dinner goes wrong—you break your favorite glass or plate, for example. Selective abstraction pounces on the misfortune and begins to weave a new story about you and the day you just experienced, one that convinces you the day wasn't so great after all, you're a klutz who always ruins things, and nothing goes well for you. All of the positive moments in the day up to that point get overlaid with this new story, which is all about you and the doom that's sure to come your way. This is what I'm referring to as the victim mindset.

One of the most insidious aspects of this mindset is the manufacture of proof where none exists. For example, we might selectively list all of the times we were overlooked at work while ignoring our ample accolades and triumphs, telling ourselves we're simply fated to fail in our career. In essence, we're creating a new myth about ourselves, and mythology always entails monsters and mysterious forces beyond our control. This is trauma's master stroke—convincing us that it's our destiny to be on the receiving end of more trauma (from God's wrath, fate's whims, or the cruelty of people in whom we placed our trust).

It would be terrible enough if people suffering from this type of victim mindset just avoided engaging in life altogether, but it's typically far more damaging. An internalized victim requires an internalized persecutor, and it's this persecuting aspect of the traumatized mind that confirms negative biases against us and engages in self-sabotage. How many of us have persecutors living within us? How many of us suffer from a constant narrative of negative self-talk? How many of us accept preventable problems as if they were predetermined? How many of us say "It serves you right" whenever something painful happens to us? We don't do this because we like to suffer; we do this because trauma has tricked us into accepting a false story about the world and who we are in it.

When we start to live with lots of blinders and with fewer boundaries to keep us safe, threats to our health and happiness are everywhere. They usually don't take the shape of the monsters our stories might tell us are out there just waiting to eat us; typically they're more like cigarettes and alcohol, missed opportunities, reckless driving, skipped checkups and missed doctor visits, and so on. Most of these threats are avoidable, but trauma convinces us we don't have much choice in the matter.

It can be difficult to fight mythology head on, but if we understand how trauma enacts these types of blinders, it becomes a lot easier not to buy into the nightmare. Life is hard enough as it is without convincing ourselves it will never be any better. We can learn to recognize when imposter truths are working to spread the trauma virus everywhere we look, and we can counter with the right antidotes.

ANTIDOTE: *Changing the Channel*

Life is stressful enough without having to deal with brains that get carried away with themselves. Sometimes we encounter subjects so distressing that our brains refuse to let go of them, and this is certainly common when it comes to brains inhabited by trauma. We can get caught up in endless cognitive loops ("I'm going to lose my job. . . . What in the world am I going to do?"), as if recycling the same thought repeatedly were conducive to solving problems. In such situations, the anxiety centers in our brain take over, commandeer our internal dialogue, and start cranking out higher levels of negative affect, feeling, and emotion. Fortunately, we can apply some practical techniques to help change the channel.

- One set of tactics involves shifting attention to things that are mundane, interesting, or humorous. Examples include noticing as many details as we can about a clock on the wall, watching an engrossing documentary, or rewatching our favorite movie from adolescence. These choices can stop the freight train of thoughts that might otherwise barrel on and block productive thoughts and even the sleep we need. After the momentum changes, we can often steer our thoughts more easily than before.

- If that doesn't work, we can try shifting our attention to something unpleasant or noxious. This option isn't as fun, but it can be highly

effective in bringing current thoughts to a halt, no matter how stubborn they might be. One example is making a music playlist that consists entirely of music you absolutely hate. Although miserable in its own right, this technique makes it nearly impossible to pay attention to anything else, and it's a highly effective method to hit the reset button on your thoughts.

- If you need something a little more drastic, dunking your head in cold water will usually do the trick. This technique triggers what's called the *mammalian dive reflex*, known not only for stopping thoughts but also for promoting a sense of calm.

It's inevitable that our brains will get carried away and stuck on one channel for far longer than we want them to, but it's also true that we can do something about it.

MY OWN LIMBIC FIRESTORM

The shock and sadness that hit me after my brother's suicide scorched everything in their path. I was angry with myself, and my self-confidence was shot. I worried about other people constantly, especially about losing them. I felt anxious and plagued with all manner of concerns and frustrations. In short, the trauma of losing my brother utterly changed my thoughts.

I can attest to how easily trauma creates an ominous internal landscape, leaving us suspicious of the outside world and doubtful of our place in it, while also placing greater emphasis upon our own negative memories and fogging up anything positive we might try to recall. Trauma is like the giant on the other end of the seesaw; it can leave us feeling stuck, stranded, and out of touch with any sense of solid ground.

Even so, with help and self-care, we can tilt the seesaw back to earth. For me, that also involved trusting in a sense of innate goodness and believing it was honorable, worthwhile, and good to devote oneself to helping other people. That's what led me to change the direction of my life and apply to medical school.

CHAPTER 11

The Limbic System

Our bodies are composed of different systems to accomplish the various functions necessary for life. For example, a system dedicated to movement allows us to walk, pick up a glass of water, breathe, or adjust the size of our pupils to let in more light. Another example is the endocrine system, which controls hormones in our bloodstreams that carry millions of different messages throughout the body.

The system I want to talk about in this chapter spans many vital areas of the brain and has the most to do with emotion. Logical matters are important to humans—counting and understanding directions to travel from one place to another, for example—but our experience of life is defined by the limbic system. Logic can fill in parts of our story, but the heart of life is rooted in the limbic system—in our joy, pride, sadness, shame, and so on.

It's no surprise, then, that the limbic system is crucial to forming and storing memories. In fact, the parts of the brain that determine our memories are actually parts of the limbic system. This speaks deeply to how we become who we are as human beings. The limbic system decides what's important in life—what we remember and how we remember it. Whenever we think about our lives by linking our memories—smiling, wincing, crying, or laughing as we do so—we're having a profoundly limbic experience. Emotions make memories, and memories evoke emotions.

Americans alive when President John F. Kennedy was assassinated in Dallas almost always remember where they were when they learned the news. The same is true for the 9/11 attacks. Our brains encode memories of all sorts, but they tend to remain vivid for a lot longer the more negative the event was to us. This makes a lot of sense when you think about it through the lens of evolutionary fitness. It might not matter to my future survival just where I was when 9/11 happened (my old studio apartment), but it might be helpful to remember the surroundings where I was mugged so that I can try to avoid harm in the future.

Thankfully, it's not just the bad stuff that causes us to lay down such strong memories. My paternal grandmother used to talk about being woken up as a child by her parents to go outside and bang pots and pans when World War I ended. It was such an exceptional event for her—making noise in the middle of the night, with the whole neighborhood participating joyously—that she still recalled that night with marvel more than seventy years later. We all have clear memories of positive things, too: the day our child was born, the return of a loved one from battle, the news that the chemotherapy is working.

The limbic system cares quite a bit about the power of emotions. These emotions determine the strength of our memories but not without bias. Sure, what we value most about life is important, but remembering the bad stuff is what's going to keep us alive. We humans and our immediate ancestors lived as hunter-gatherers for hundreds of thousands of years. Whenever we entered a new valley or forest, it was nice to remember which berries, roots, and mushrooms were the tastiest and the most filling, but it was absolutely vital to recall which ones gave us diarrhea and made us vomit.

This explains why trauma affects our memories so deeply. Our limbic system tries to protect us, but that protection can become colored with fear and shame. Without our logical systems in play, our memories can get twisted into beliefs that are simply untrue. This tendency is supposed to have our best interests in mind, but far too often it results in poor health and unhappiness.

AFFECT, FEELING, AND EMOTION

These three words are often used interchangeably, but I want to pull them apart here to illustrate how trauma works on the limbic system. Let's begin with affect. By *affect*, I'm referring to an internal experience created without our conscious choice in the matter. Affect comes on automatically, and it can take over control of our brain and body. We can certainly experience affect from positive events, such as turning a corner and seeing someone we like very much—the rush of sudden happiness can be a pleasant surprise. Whatever was going on in our brain before—thinking about the grocery list, for example—immediately vanishes and gets replaced with that happiness, changing us from head to toe. That change might only last a couple of minutes, but it might also lift our spirits for days.

> Our brains were built to move fast because
> the world around us moves fast.

Although positive changes in affect are wonderful to experience, negative changes are a different story. In addition to other physical changes, negative affects such as fear and shame prepare the brain's memory mechanisms to record the event, but the recording is filtered to favor safety and survival. Anyone who's been publicly embarrassed in middle school or high school can relate. Imagine you're doing a math problem in front of the entire class. While you're working away on the blackboard, you accidentally drop the piece of chalk, and when you bend over to pick it up, your pants rip. Everyone points at you and laughs. Not only will you be far more likely to remember the embarrassing experience but also chances are you'll want to avoid that classroom in particular and maybe even working in front of people in general. It might seem like a silly example, but imagine how that rush of the initial affect (shame) and the resultant memories could get out of hand, especially for a child. Instead of remembering how well you solved the math problem on the board, your teacher's approving nods, and so on, you're given everything a child needs to develop a fear of public speaking.

Next, *feeling* occurs a split second after affect arrives. In this usage, feeling refers to how we relate the affect to ourselves—in the example above, "People always make fun of me" or "Nobody likes me." Emotion occurs a split second after feeling comes up and broadens the experience to include others. Maybe one of the kids laughing in the front row of the class—a classmate who had previously been nice—is of a different ethnicity or gender or income bracket. In this case, emotion might try to convince us that this particular person is directly related to our affect of shame and our resultant feelings about ourselves. This is how negative emotions can result in prejudices (or strengthen them), blame ("My mother shouldn't have made me wear these pants"), or other generalizations ("God is punishing me").

Affect leads to feeling; feeling leads to emotion. This cascade evolved to enhance our survival, but nowadays it can lead to distorted messages that don't benefit us in the future. This is the limbic system at work. Safety and survival at all costs means that logic, clear perspective, and accurate, comprehensive memories far too often take a backseat.

Our brains were built to move fast because the world around us moves fast. We don't have to stop and think about every little thing that happens in our environment—our brains take shortcuts; they make automatic leaps all the time. This also happens with daily activities to which we don't pay much attention—brushing our teeth, for example. If we had to think about every little step involved in the process—locating our toothbrush, picking it up, squeezing out the toothpaste just so, opening our mouth, and so on—we'd probably brush our teeth a lot less often and have way more cavities because brushing our teeth would entail too much work. If you're like me, you often finish brushing your teeth without being all that conscious of the process. In fact, you probably spend that time thinking about a dozen different things. In those few short minutes (depending on how thorough you are about your dental care), your brain makes hundreds of decisions along the way, but you don't have to consciously deliberate about any of them.

Unfortunately, trauma has a lot to say about how our limbic system and the affect-feeling-emotion cascade play out in our lives. Where we go, who we talk to, who we avoid, what chances we take and what opportunities we shy away from, what we think in our heads repeatedly about ourselves, how we take care of our bodies, what we automatically believe that we wouldn't believe if we stopped and really thought about it—this short list is just the tip of the trauma iceberg.

Trauma leaves us with fewer resources
to fight the effects of trauma.

Trauma is sort of like a windup child's toy that springs wildly from one place to another, out of control. After it gets going, we can't predict where it will end up—we just know that it will have knocked some things over by the time it stops. When it comes to trauma we're along for the ride, and we often arrive at places we'd never decide to go, with dangers we never asked for. I wish I could use the "bull-in-a-china-shop" metaphor for trauma, but it doesn't fit as well. The bull can do a lot of damage, but the damage is hard to miss, and the cause of the damage is fairly obvious.

In reality, trauma is way more secretive than a giant bull or a crazy, spinning toy. Without our ever knowing it, trauma hijacks our limbic system, twists our memories, and changes our brain. We feel, think, decide, and act in ways we never would have before. We become different people, often without being able to track that difference. It's the ultimate sabotage.

Trauma begets more trauma. Trauma leaves us with fewer resources to fight the effects of trauma. Those resources are both internal and external—a decreased sense of well-being, energy diverted to maintain hypervigilance, supportive relationships we avoid or don't foster, the dream career we let go of because we're afraid of failure, the demoralizing impact of negative self-talk that tries to convince us bad things always happen to us, the consequences of dangerous situations we put ourselves in because we don't believe we deserve to be safe, and so on.

The limbic system is not the problem; trauma is the problem. Trauma is incredibly powerful, but it's not invincible, and the limbic system can also be a potent ally with benign and healing capabilities. By expressing compassion for ourselves and others, and by allowing the compassion of others to take root in ourselves, we can heal from the ravages of trauma and change our lives for the better.

ANTIDOTE: *Finding Supportive Environments*
We all need to experience the kindness and acceptance of others. This is doubly true for those of us wounded by trauma. Make sure that you and your loved ones are nourished with caring, open environments—support groups, circles of friends, spiritual communities, and so on. Together we can help one another battle the negative loops trauma creates and foster positive cycles that promote health and happiness.

LEAPING AND LANDING

The limbic system isn't oriented to linear time. As far as the limbic system goes, whatever happened in the past might as well be happening right now in the present moment because if the affect, feeling, and emotion are strong enough, that's what it feels like. That has a lot to say about the way we make decisions. Remember that the brain is designed to make automatic leaps. Every time the brain leaps, it has to land and check its bearings—it has to take stock of where it's landed and what all of the available information means.

Trauma hijacks our limbic system and wreaks havoc.

Imagine you're driving on a highway. It's raining out, and you decide to pull off at the next exit ramp. When you do, you see a traffic light a hundred yards or so up ahead, and the light turns yellow. Without thinking much about it, your brain and body just naturally coordinate to slow the car down until you're sitting at the red light waiting for it to change. While you're waiting, you might fidget with the radio or notice details outside of the car totally unrelated to operating the vehicle—a robin in the branch of the tree nearby, for example, or the smell of the rain and wet grass. All of this goes fairly smoothly, but look what happens if we add trauma.

Maybe you were in a car accident in the rain just a couple of months back, or maybe you were hit from behind by a driver who wasn't paying attention while you waited for a light to turn green. All the leaping and landing your brain engages in now is colored with powerful memories as well as strong affects, feelings, and emotions. As soon as you turn onto the exit ramp and see the light turn yellow, you feel the anxiety in your body because you know you'll have to stop at the red light and wait. Your memory sounds the alarm because as far as it's concerned, exit ramp + rain + red light = accident. Your fear gets triggered, and your experience of the past trauma starts to play out in the present moment. Your body starts to tense up—all of those automatic driving movements involving your hands, eyes, and feet aren't so automatic anymore, and the added vigilance (tightening grip, intensely checking the rearview mirror) actually makes the possibility of another accident more likely. You miss enjoying the robin in the tree, and the smell of rain in the present confuses your worried brain trying to hold on to the difference between the present and the past, when the accident happened.

In moments of high stress like this, the limbic system has already determined that the current situation might as well be the past event that caused you the original trauma. And because the limbic system cares about safety and survival first, it throws the calendar out of the window along with logic and the ability to take in new information. This is how trauma hijacks our limbic system and wreaks havoc.

MEMORIES DON'T HOLD MEANING

Memories themselves don't contain meaning. Instead, parts of the brain called *association cortexes* integrate knowledge and experience to create meaning. Let's say I get home from work and catch a whiff of that delicious smell of cookies baking in the oven. I instantly feel good, but why? There are several pieces to this experience, the first being the pure smell of cookies baking. Another piece is that I happen to like cookies. Yet another is the expectation that my wife and daughters—the likely bakers in this scenario—will likely give me one of the tasty cookies. If I smile and ask nicely, I might even get two. I anticipate how good those cookies will taste, and my mouth starts to water. I even start to imagine how good that cold glass of milk will be with said cookies.

An area of association cortex puts all this together. My sense of the stream of this experience is simple and seamless, but that's only because areas of association cortex have made it possible. And part of how they make it possible is by integrating memories and their limbic system meanings—the affects, feelings, and emotions associated with the memories.

Imagine memories have little flags attached to them. These flags signal an area of association cortex to go out and grab the affects, feelings, and emotions that match the flags. The association cortex can then bring the memory and the limbic system meaning together, and thereby the memory is infused with life. Before that, the memory was just a piece of data; now it holds significance. This is what the brain takes into account when making its next leap forward.

The limbic system flags attached to our memories become our guideposts. They are immeasurably important. They are designed to prevent us from navigating blindly into the future, but they can just as easily lead us astray. When the flags are highly charged with negative affect, feeling, and emotion, they become less like roadside guideposts and more like roadside bombs, but that's only part of the story. They can also rewrite our maps so that we forget what we have known, making it even harder to navigate effectively. Instead of logical and limbic processes integrating in a series of controlled leaps, what happens inside of us can become more like frantic lunging, as if we were fleeing madly from pain. But the pain of the past has us springing madly toward more pain in the future.

For this reason, it's crucial that we learn how to help our brains stay calm enough to pay attention to logic, use prior knowledge, and recognize how linear time works. We must help our brains use these limbic system flags in ways that can best serve us because when the flags are more like signs twisted in the wrong direction, or bombs ready to detonate, or panic buttons that trigger more trauma responses, all the flags are going to do is propel us toward unhappy and at times dangerous outcomes.

FIRING AND WIRING

By now, "neurons that fire together wire together" has become a widely recognized aphorism. Neurons are cells in our nervous system that transmit information, and each of our brains contains more than 80 billion of them! Whenever a neural pathway is activated, all of the neurons along that pathway fire, transmitting information from the beginning of the neural string to the end. Certain molecules pass information between the neurons, which also have receptors to receive the signal so that it can be passed on. And whenever an exchange like this occurs in the neural string, the connection between all the neurons in the pathway gets stronger.

Let's use *platypus* as an example—not the unusual creature itself, but the word. If you were to say *platypus* repeatedly—200 times, for example—the chances of you thinking about that word later and even tomorrow go through the roof. Unless you're the type of person who regularly says *platypus* on purpose, the neural pathways associated with the word don't get a whole lot of use. So, if you want to get the word *platypus* stuck in your head for a while, just keep firing those neural pathways, and they'll get strong enough to wire together.

This is how we learn anything, really—our names and those of our parents, our telephone number and address, how to tie our shoes and open a book. The same process is involved with complex information as well, and this is how trauma distorts the world and ingrains its messages within us. It's how we learn that we aren't good enough, that we'll always be hurt, that the world is invariably harmful, that people who look a certain way are dangerous, that things are getting worse, that nothing ever goes right no matter how hard we try. The pathways just keep firing and getting stronger, so much so that healthier ideas and facts to the contrary get pushed into the background. I don't know if it's actually true that we are what we eat, but it's definitely true that we are what we think.

ANTIDOTE: *Wait a Minute!*

The neural pathways we engage repeatedly are difficult to counter after they get going but not impossible. That's why the battle against trauma and its consequences regularly uses the tactic of halting those pathways with a "Wait a minute!" response. That "Wait a minute!" response lets us pause, reflect, decide, and choose. Sometimes the tactic is as simple as recognizing the flags trauma has assigned to our memories—for example, a flag that says being vulnerable with others is always dangerous. If we can see flags like that for what they are, it means we can offer an alternative—for example, "I've been hurt in the past, it's true. But I didn't deserve it, I know what to look out for, and I can get close to people while also being judicious so that I don't get hurt again." That's a lot to put on one little flag, but you get the idea. Of course, switching limbic system flags doesn't happen overnight. Some messages are wired together tightly, and it takes substantial, sustained effort to counter them. This is why old habits are hard to break, but it's also how we're able to create new habits of our own choosing—habits that help us heal from trauma and protect us from more trauma happening in the future as we do our best to live our lives to the fullest.

I Have to Kill the Rats

Several years ago, I took care of an elderly woman trying to get rid of rats. The rats weren't in her house; they were in her sinuses. She kept coming to the ER of the hospital where I worked to ask us to get rid of them. The rats had lived in her sinuses for years and years, she said. Sometimes it wasn't that big of a deal to her, but sometimes she became extremely upset and frantic, yelling over and over, "I have to kill the rats!" to the point where she required sedation to keep her and everyone else safe.

This unfortunate woman could never understand how everyone else could remain so calm. How could we just go about our business when we should be just as worried as she was about her terrible rat problem? Why weren't we calling the specialists and preparing an operating room to remove them? At times like these, the only specialist the staff ever called was a psychiatrist, often me.

It was almost impossible to make any connection with her. She was suspicious of everyone, and she often heard voices telling her how the rats were creeping out of her sinuses and traveling around her body doing secret damage. She described them in a nightmarish way—dirty and twitching and aggressive. The rats were inside of her, she couldn't control them, and they were always hurting her or getting ready to hurt her. All of this made me their accomplice because I knew all about them yet did nothing. How could she trust me, or anyone else in the hospital, when we pretended it wasn't happening? At best, she considered us callous and incompetent; at worst, she believed we might have put the rats there in the first place and were laughing behind her back.

As I got to know her a little better, I found out that the rats had been in her sinuses since her teens, when some terrible things had happened in her life. She told me how awful it was that the rats came at the same time as the loss and abuse she suffered, but she hadn't considered that maybe the rats were there because of the loss and abuse. I was never able to get her to take medicine—she was put off and even insulted by the idea. In general, she was exasperated with me and found me entirely unhelpful.

I didn't know what to do to help her. At some point, I decided to level with her. I agreed that my expertise was limited and that I knew nothing whatsoever about getting rats out of sinuses. I also agreed that it was entirely possible that I knew nothing whatsoever about much of anything, except for maybe one thing. I could see that she wasn't sleeping well, and I knew I could help her with that. It took a while, but she'd been suffering quite a bit from insomnia, so she eventually accepted the medicine that I recommended.

I want to be clear that I didn't trick her into taking medicine for a different purpose, such as reducing the voices she heard. I wanted to help her get some sleep—rats or no rats. I was surprised that I even got that far with her, but one night as I was leaving the hospital, I checked in on the woman in her hospital room. She was lying in bed, half asleep, looking over at me.

"How are you doing?" I asked.

"The rats are sleeping," she replied, as calmly as could be.

This is a powerful example of just how overwhelmed our brains can become with the shock of trauma. This woman wasn't born with delusions of rats in her sinuses; that only happened after all of the horrible abuse she suffered. The fearful parts of our brains create stories in an effort to make sense of the world and sometimes as a last-ditch attempt to regain some hope of control. Sometimes the stories are about how bad we are; or how much the world has it in for us; or how we've disappointed God, who is punishing us. And if a person happens to be susceptible to certain neurological conditions, and the trauma is severe enough, sometimes the stories include voices and visions.

I believe this woman was desperately trying to get the trauma out of her. For some reason, her unbearable memories and feelings took the form of rats who lived in her sinuses, and going to the ER to remove the rats gave her something to do about it. But this approach only made everything worse. We weren't able to fix her rat problem, and she felt more alone, distrustful, and alienated every time she visited the hospital.

I think admitting my cluelessness helped her feel a little less alone—enough, at least, to stop seeing me as an adversary—enough to receive a little help. We both knew how miserable the insomnia made her, and it turns out she didn't need to kill the rats to finally get some peace and rest. The rats needed sleep, too. It might have been the first break from her trauma in years.

⇥**REFLECTION:** Think about a time when you believed a story about yourself or the world that wasn't true. It doesn't have to be anything as dramatic as this woman and the rats who lived in her sinuses, just something you learned at an early age that didn't (or doesn't) serve you later in adulthood. Think about how certain memories get attached to affects, feelings, and emotions that don't always have a lot to do with the present moment. Lastly, see if you can determine which flags trauma has placed on those memories and which flags you might replace them with—new flags that promote your well-being and your ability to avoid future trauma and better guide your life forward.

CHAPTER 12

The Physical and Mental Ravages of Trauma

Our brains don't work without our bodies, and our bodies don't work without our brains. The connection between them isn't just about a neck that holds it all together; it's about all the information that passes back and forth through that neck. This information can take the form of nerve impulses that travel through the spinal cord to every part of our bodies and back to our brains, or it could look more like the hormones certain organs release into our bloodstreams. All of the perceptual data we could ever imagine is codified and delivered in such a way that the body and brain can work together for the good of the whole.

The brain-body connection is like an extremely complex network of roads governed by a set of rules that makes the whole network function. On actual roads, we have rules for how fast you can go, who gets to go first at an intersection, how much noise a vehicle is allowed to make, and so on. Similarly, on the brain-to-body and body-to-brain roads, there are rules for how fast our nerves and the bloodstream can spread their messages, which messages get priority, and which ones signal the loudest. Ideally, that is.

Imagine that the rules governing communication inside of us are changed such that pain and distress signals are given a blatant advantage across the board. The pain and distress signals would travel faster, get higher priority on express pathways, and deliver their messages more emphatically when reaching their destinations (either in the brain or in the body). When the basic rules of the network change in this way, our entire internal environment changes. It becomes biased toward the negative and extrasensitive to anything that resembles a danger signal.

Salience is an important word in neurobiology and in psychiatry. It describes the degree to which a particular thought, feeling, or perception stands out above others. Adjustments in salience involve shifts in brain chemistry, alterations in protein building blocks, and a whole lot more. These adjustments can remodel the brain in a dramatic and not necessarily improved manner, just as if someone remodeled your house to have dim lighting, fire alarms that go off unnecessarily, and a large pit in the living room that holds a couple of alligators. Trauma adjusts salience, and these adjustments can amplify emotional danger signals (negative affect, feeling, and emotion) as well as physical danger signals (pain). This is how trauma burdens us with additional suffering of all sorts.

INFLAMMATION AND CHRONIC PAIN

Inflammation naturally occurs in the body to help us recover from injuries and fight off infections, but inflammation can also be caused by trauma. The earlier our trauma is in life or the more severe it is, the more potent its inflammatory effects. This occurs because trauma and its accomplices create stress, and our body understands stress as a key to signal inflammation, but without a specific injury or infection to work on, that inflammation just travels around our circulatory system looking for something to do. When you hear that stress causes health problems such as heart disease and cancer, this is why.

So, trauma changes the rules of the road, alters how the brain and body communicate, and turns our internal environment into hostile terrain where inflammation and pain gain way more traction than they normally would. *Fibromyalgia*—a disorder characterized by chronic pain, fatigue, and memory loss—is just one example with an established connection to trauma. Unfortunately, fibromyalgia and many forms of chronic pain are often treated without much consideration for trauma or the brain-body connection.

Inflammation creates a cascade of dysfunction.

Trauma promotes pain, pain increases suffering, and suffering makes us desperate to soothe our pain, whatever form it takes. Sadly, we're seeing this terrible cycle play out on a larger societal level with the opiate epidemic. Far too many people suffer from emotional and physical pain without understanding where it comes from or how to address it, which means that external forms of soothing aren't just appealing but often irresistible. People who become addicted to opiates didn't necessarily seek them out to get high. Too many are desperately reaching out for anything to help them suffer less. Too many find opiates as false relief when they are prescribed for something else, such as an injury or surgery. Unfortunately, the relief from opiates is short-lived and requires larger and larger doses for people to receive the same effect. Eventually, people caught in this cycle have to dose just in order not to experience the pain of withdrawal from the opiate. It's a terrible and tragic loop that costs many thousands of lives every year.

ANTIDOTE: *Reducing Tension*

Anxiety is unpleasant to experience in multiple ways, including how it signals the brain to create more muscle tension in the body, which, in turn, tells the brain there's something to be anxious about. Unless we find a way to intervene, this unpleasant cycle can take on a life of its own.

One common place this cycle manifests in the body is in the gastrointestinal (GI) system, often creating or contributing to irritable bowel syndrome (IBS). Another common place is in the chest, where it can lead to a sensation of not being able to breathe in enough air because the muscles between the ribs tighten up, thereby decreasing the lungs' capacity for expansion. We also hold a lot of tension in major muscle groups, such as our neck, shoulders, back, behind, and thighs. This tension promotes more pain and poor physical alignment, which affect other muscles, tissue, and nerves.

Progressive muscle relaxation can allow us both to recognize and relieve the muscle tension that is part of the anxiety-in-the-brain/tension-in-the-body cycle. To expand on an antidote I offered in chapter 3, one common technique I recommend is the bedtime strategy of starting at the toes and working your way up your body by slowly tensing a set of muscles and then relaxing them. This method begins with the toes and ends with the forehead and scalp, and you can vary the duration (and repetition) of each sequence depending on your needs. This technique shifts the chemistry in the brain and body to a more relaxed state, and it can inform us where we're holding stress in our bodies. Whenever I use this method, I often find places I'm holding tension in my body I wasn't aware of before. The added benefit is that I'm able to bring more attention to those parts during the day and try to bring them more relaxation through stretching or self-massage. It's remarkable how much difference a self-administered, two-minute shoulder massage can make!

You can also add imagery to this antidote, especially at night. As I mentioned before, imagery that employs as many senses as possible works best. With a little practice, this technique becomes a lot easier to perform, even to the point of being automatic at bedtime. We can also revisit our favorite imagery during the day to ease whatever tension we feel starting to build up in our bodies. I regularly take a quick trip to the beach in my mind for this reason.

AUTOIMMUNE DISEASES

Increased inflammation has been shown to affect our immune system, which is responsible for fighting off both external and internal intruders—bacteria, viruses, and mutated cancer cells, for example. Without a well-functioning immune system, we become highly vulnerable to all sorts of threats we otherwise would not have to worry about. Because the array of dangers facing us has been so diverse over the course of our evolution, our immune system has become exceptionally complicated to meet these challenges.

Think of the immune system as a large army. The army includes a command hierarchy, an array of soldiers dedicated to different tasks, and a wide range of weapons and equipment. The immune system's army spans from microscopic cells to large organs. It includes the bone marrow, which creates our blood cells; legions of white blood cells that maintain vigilance against threats; molecules that spread throughout the bloodstream; lymph nodes; and organs such as our skin, intestines, and spleen. It has a command hierarchy so complicated that science is constantly learning new insights into exactly how it functions. It can eat or stab invaders, poison them, expel them outright, disarm them, or outwit them. The immune system can also see through camouflage and has the ability to access ancient data to solve present-day problems.

When such a powerful and complex system goes awry, the damage can be incalculable. Inflammation creates a cascade of dysfunction that triggers the immune system, confuses it, and can cause it to turn its weapons against us. And when the immune system turns against the body and brain it's designed to protect, it can lead to low-level symptoms such as fatigue, nausea, increased pain, rashes, and hair loss, or it can result in more impactful and large-scale autoimmune disorders. These can include rheumatoid arthritis, lupus, multiple sclerosis, psoriasis, and Crohn's disease. Many diseases of the thyroid, skin, and blood vessels are autoimmune in nature, and no part of the body or brain is beyond the reach of autoimmune assault. Trauma and stress lead to inflammation, which increases the likelihood of problems in our immune system, resulting in impairment of various physical and mental functions that cause additional suffering and can, in fact, put our life at risk.

EPIGENETICS AND CHILDHOOD STRESS

Epigenetics is the study and science of how events in our lives can turn genes on or off. We aren't simply passive carriers of ancestral DNA—our experiences determine which of our traits are active and which remain dormant. In addition to trauma-driven epigenetic changes being associated with some autoimmune diseases, childhood traumatic stress has been shown to increase inflammation in adulthood as well as the likelihood of autoimmune diseases.

ACCELERATED AGING

Neurobiological studies have also found that trauma actually accelerates our aging. It's natural for our DNA to change as we age—these changes are markers for the degeneration of our brain and body, which ultimately leads to death. They decrease many aspects of our functioning and eventually lead to us dying from an age-related cause if we live long enough. Studies show that trauma makes naturally occurring DNA changes progress further than what would be expected at a given age, such that a person is actually older than their lived age!

We don't have to give trauma a free pass.

We cannot calculate the projected loss of time and quality of life for a particular person, but we make estimates based upon life experiences and mental health variables. For example, we know that childhood trauma plays a significant role, as does the severity of whatever trauma a person experiences. We also know that suffering from depression is a factor when it comes to aging, and depression is often associated with trauma. This doesn't mean, of course, that everyone who is depressed has experienced trauma, but trauma makes it more likely that a person will suffer from depression.

NEW NORMALS AREN'T SO NORMAL

Trauma creates a new normal in our brain and body that often includes afflictions and disadvantages that weren't there before. These could take the form of more pain and illness, or they could look more like foregone opportunities, depression, and lost years off an otherwise long and healthy life. Trauma tries to sneak all of this under the radar so that we forget what we wanted out of life—our goals fade behind us in the distance, our mental and physical health decline, and all manner of ideas previously unacceptable become part of our new normal. It's as if a shadow eclipses our view of the future, and if we simply stand by, the shadow grows darker and larger all around us.

It's true that the outcomes of trauma are regularly grim, but it doesn't have to be that way. The more we learn about trauma and how it works in our lives, the more we can counter it. We don't simply have to suffer from trauma's new normal; we don't have to give trauma a free pass in our lives as individuals or as a society. We can turn the tide toward a *chosen* normal— one of greater ease, health, and happiness.

You Can't Help It—You're Italian!

At one time, I had an urgent-care part of my practice in which I saw people who were frequently hospitalized. They came in for regular appointments, but they could also just show up if they weren't doing well. One of these patients was an older woman who abided by a sense of propriety from a bygone era, and she dressed so conservatively that I wondered if she got her clothes from a costume shop.

The woman heard voices almost constantly. The voices told her that she wasn't safe, that she was in danger from aliens and poisons and all manner of other threats, including men. In particular, she interpreted any arm or hand gesture from a man as sexual in nature—waving down a cab, for example, or the thumbs-up gesture. When she confided the "true" meanings of these motions, they were way more graphic than you'd imagine. I was fairly certain I could help her. First of all, she rarely went out, and when she did, she avoided looking at men. And I was able to help her with the voices partly through changes in her medicine.

I told her I would try my best not to move my arms or hands when we were together, but it would be difficult because—as the old adage says—Italians talk with their hands, and I am no exception to the stereotype. She wasn't Italian, but she appreciated the joke. I told her that even if I ever did accidentally make a gesture, I would not mean it to be sexual, and I routinely sat on my hands to make sure I wouldn't alarm her. Sure enough, at some point she was doing a lot better, and she began to express surprising insights, including some about ways she'd found to counter the voices, which had bothered her for ages. Well, this made me quite happy, and as I was excitedly responding, I saw a look of horror cross her face.

Then I noticed that my hands were up in the air, both of them gesturing wildly. It wasn't my best clinical moment.

I sat on my hands quickly and apologized profusely as my patient looked at me with shock and fear. But then her expression softened, and she said, with the gentle remonstrating humor one of my aunts might have used when I was growing up, that I couldn't help it because I was Italian. We laughed about it, I continued apologizing, and I did a much better job of sitting on my hands from there on out. I'm happy to say that she kept improving and was hospitalized far less often than she previously was.

I never learned whether something sexually traumatizing happened to this woman. She certainly didn't feel safe around men, and she suffered from a debilitating illness that imposed frightening voices wherever she went. She was lonely and afraid at home, and it was even worse when she went out of the house, but she had a prevailing desire to feel better and to become healthier. Fortunately, she also had a sense of humor. Whatever trauma happened to her earlier in life wasn't able to eradicate her willingness to take chances in order to suffer less—it's how she came to my clinic in the first place, and it's how she endured my shortcomings as a caregiver.

REFLECTION: Think of your own resilience in the face of obstacles or threats (perceived or actual). What was it in you that kept you going? What helped you readjust or recover after setbacks? What qualities saw you through to the other side?

PART FOUR

HOW WE CAN BEAT TRAUMA — TOGETHER

---

*After all that I've been through, all that's been
done to me, I am still trustworthy. I do right
by people because it's hard in this world.*

K.S.T.

CHAPTER 13

The Way Home

L ike you, I'm a lot of people wrapped up into one. I'm a curious person as well as an impatient one. I'm a father, a husband, a friend, a doctor, a psychiatrist, and so on. I'm also someone who's been changed by trauma. Like most of you reading this, I've been affected by some significant difficulties in my own life and the lives of people I care about.

All of us have unique stories with their own idiosyncratic plots, peaks, troughs, and trials. Although commonalities run through them—familiar foes, for example—none of our stories are the same. Each of us is as rare and fascinating as any natural treasure—Mount Everest, the Serengeti, Niagara Falls—and as precious and worthy of care as any endangered species. In truth, that's what we are. Each of us is a precious rarity of one. Each of us matters.

Trauma makes this easy to forget. It makes it easy to forget about ourselves and about each other. Trauma tells us to turn a blind eye not only to suffering but also to health and happiness. Trauma is the great eraser—the thief who steals what's most precious, the virus that makes us forget everything about what it means to be human. Trauma subverts our compassion, tears our communities apart, and turns humanity into a far-off memory. Compassion, community, and humanity come only from learning more about ourselves and others, expressing our truths, and listening to one another with open hearts and minds.

Trauma tries to convince us that compassion, community, and humanity aren't possible. It tells us that health, happiness, and true human connection are pipe dreams—mere fantasies. Trauma mocks our fundamental urges to learn, express, and listen to each other in order to make a better life for all of us, and it does so in secret by camouflaging its voice and disguising its true intent.

I want that to change—as quickly as possible—and this book is my change agent. My hope is that I've helped you in some way to understand trauma, recognize how it works, and motivated you to do something about it. I also hope I've convinced you trauma is a problem for each and every one of us, and we all must work together to counter trauma's assault on compassion, community, and humanity.

Trauma is hurting us right now—you, me, our children and friends, our neighbors, our so-called enemies . . . everyone. Trauma is eating away at our towns, cities, countries, and continents. Trauma isn't something to look into later—it is happening right now. If an innocent child were being threatened in front of you right now, you'd want to do something about it—you wouldn't even stop to put thoughts or words to it being the right thing to do. That's the same heart-felt urgency we need when it comes to trauma.

FIVE CRITICAL LINKS

Here are five positive links in the chain for changing your life and the world for the better. Remembering these five points will help reorient you back to the north star of healing from trauma.

- **KNOWLEDGE.** In large part, this book is all about offering more knowledge to help you understand trauma better, learn how trauma and its accomplices operate, and inform your decisions going forward.

- **POWER.** *Scientia potentia est,* or "knowledge is power." What we learn empowers us to enact desired changes in our lives and the world.

- **HEALING.** Ideally, at the top of our list of desired changes is healing. For healing to take place, individuals and societies must use their power for good.

- **HOPE.** Healing brings hope, and hope is one of the best medicines we have against this epidemic of trauma. Hope reminds us that regardless of what has happened to us, we can do something about it. We can get better, and so can the world.

- **URGENCY.** Part of the knowledge link that kicked off this chain is understanding that we're in crisis. Trauma is already at work, and the stakes have been high for some time. Hope is also knowledge in that we come to realize the promise of a better life isn't something to take lightly. We need to do something about it, and now.

This chain could begin with any of these links, but I like to place knowledge first because of the way trauma operates in secret. Even when the causes of trauma are dramatic and obvious, its consequences mostly play out in secret. Trauma deploys its accomplices—especially shame—often without us being aware of how it all works, which is why it's so important to arm ourselves with knowledge. I hope the time and effort you've put into reading this book have led you to understand trauma in a new way. This book is intended to describe trauma's complexity and its strength, and I've tried to elucidate what trauma does to us and our societies as well as how the terrible cycles arising from trauma spread from individual to society and from society to individual. And I hope I've convinced you to do your part in healing from trauma because the cascade of trauma isn't going to stop until enough of us work together to do something about it.

Our understanding and resolve will help us define ourselves and our tomorrows. There's no mystery as to why we must change. If trauma goes unchecked, we don't have much of a shot at the justice and safety and basic rights most of us value and crave. Anything we can do to lessen the impact of trauma is, in itself, generative. Using our knowledge, power, healing, and hope in an urgent way is generative, too.

Knowing what you now know about trauma, take stock of your own experiences and outline a new understanding of how trauma has affected you. It doesn't have to be direct, either—maybe you've gained new knowledge about how trauma has affected your spouse, or maybe you understand a little better how societal traumas have affected you and your family (think about the issues discussed in chapter 8—racism, for example). You could try this antidote as a writing exercise for yourself or as a way to share with someone you trust. Communicating new knowledge like this solidifies new understandings about our lived experience, and it can help other people to comprehend theirs in a new way as well. It's just one more practical way we can work to heal from trauma and reclaim the compassion, community, and humanity that are naturally ours.

ALLIES, ANGELS, AND DEVILS

I want to reiterate here that we're not meant to face trauma alone. To that end, it's important to rely on allies—family and friends, doctors and therapists, pets, support groups, medicine, gardens, you name it. By this point, I hope I've made the *togetherness* aspect of trauma work (especially in the form of compassion, community, and humanity) clear. It's crucial that we develop the inclination to rely on the wisdom and kindness of others, and I have learned not to underestimate the power of the warm hand and the written word. Other people remind us of who we are, help us uncover our true maps, and advise us as we chart new courses to where we want to be in life.

When trauma hits, it affects all aspects of our brains, which means altered perceptions, calculations, and conclusions.

That being said, we also need to learn to be better allies to ourselves. This can also take many forms—positive self-talk, thoughtful self-care, self-confidence, self-assertion, and the habit of making well-thought-out choices about our health, careers, and the people we spend time with.

Sometimes I think about the old cartoons I used to watch when I was a kid. A lot of it was just mindless entertainment, but there was often great music in the background as well as the occasional life lesson. I remember more than once seeing an angel and a devil appear on the shoulders of a character considering whether to do a bad thing. The angel and devil would each state their case, argue with each other (and often physically fight), and the person would ultimately choose, with predictable outcomes. As a child, it wasn't lost on me that something similar was going on in me, too.

Should I get into the cookie jar while my mom was in the other room on the phone? Push my brother from behind because he was playing with a toy I wanted? I'd weigh the pros and cons, go through the options, and sometimes even picture an angel on one of my shoulders and a devil on the other. I don't think it's any accident that the creators of those old cartoons presented it that way because I think most of us can relate. Each of us might have one mind, but it has different facets.

Few of us experience actual personas such as angels and devils inside of us or voices that set forth clear, contradictory cases, but this is because the process happens below the threshold of consciousness. Our minds are very much like icebergs. The conscious part—the part we're aware of, the part with which we experience the world and navigate our days—is the part of the iceberg above water we can see. However, most of what goes on in our brains is below water—that massive bulk below the surface. It's where our fears, shame, and biases most strongly play out.

When trauma hits, it affects all aspects of our brains, which means altered perceptions, calculations, and conclusions. Remember, too, that all of this happens without our knowing it. Remember the ice cream example? We might be thinking one thing, but when it comes time to make a decision, a part of us below the surface sets forth a surprising conclusion—"You can't do this" just as we're about to walk into an interview for a job we really want; "I should stay—it'll be different this time" after we've already decided to leave an unhealthy relationship; or "Just this once" when considering an addictive habit we gave up months or years ago.

I think this internal tug-of-war is familiar to most of us. It can be confusing and gut-wrenching. On one side are the healthy angels, who want us to think through our decisions and take care of ourselves; on the other, the devils, who tell us we should give up, not challenge ourselves, stop caring, be blindly hopeful, stay in bed, or whatever it is that confirms we don't deserve what's good in life. Trauma creates more and more of these devils, empowers them, and turns the tug-of-war into an uneven contest full of disappointment, pain, sadness, and shame. Meanwhile, we're the ones in the middle getting yanked around while the devils pull us closer and closer to the muddy pit.

ANTIDOTE: *Playing Tug-of-War*

If this analogy works for you, and you sometimes feel caught in the middle of a tug-of-war between healthy and unhealthy impulses, try this out: Make it conscious. Bring the process to the surface and acknowledge the conflict going on within you. If it helps, imagine an angel on one shoulder and a devil on the other (or other characters of whatever type, depending on the nature of the conflict). The most important part of this practice is to accept and voice the conflict of opinions inside of you. In this way, you can imagine yourself in the middle without giving up your power. You can hear what each "pull" has to say, determine what value it has in a conscious way, reflect, and ultimately choose what's best for you (as opposed to having it be chosen for you).

Because of the survival-based negativity bias I've mentioned previously in the book, trauma already has a leg up in the game. We see this play out strongly whenever we hold different opinions about emotionally charged topics, especially when they relate to what we think about ourselves. *"Am I a good enough parent?"* for example, or *"Do I deserve to ask for that promotion?"* When questions like these come up, it's not the best time for the loudest opinions to win because they usually come from the traumatized aspects of ourselves, which are afraid and ashamed.

Exercises such as the ones offered in this chapter can help us to separate the wheat from the chaff. By pausing, bringing awareness to the different messages going on inside of us, and taking our time to decide what's true and what's not, we can make sure we've got our best interests in mind. It's not okay to just go along for the ride because sometimes our drivers are confused and don't know where they're going. We want our best selves in the driver's seat. That's how we heal from trauma and guide ourselves to greater compassion, community, and humanity.

ANTIDOTE: *Enhancing Awareness*

Our minds are often busy, speedy, and full of contradictory information that can be difficult to track. Here's a shorthand version of two well-known, reliable practices to slow down and clarify the mind that have been around for thousands of years:

- **MEDITATION.** Countless books and videos promote meditation, and there are as many ways to meditate as there are books and videos about it. One simple technique you can do anywhere is to just take measured breaths in and out, paying attention to how the air fills your lungs and then how your lungs feel as the air leaves your body. Doing this repeatedly (often by counting up to ten and then starting over) is a time-honored method for honing your awareness. It helps to do this practice in a quiet place with few distractions, but sometimes just taking a short walk outside will do the trick (as long as you're paying attention and not texting or surfing the web on your phone, that is).

- **SELF-INQUIRY.** This is a practice of directing your attention inward and becoming purposefully interested in what's going on inside of you. Self-inquiry goes well with meditation, and both practices are often used in tandem. We're regularly unaware of the thoughts that guide our actions and even less aware of the thoughts and reasoning beneath those thoughts. Self-inquiry is basically getting curious about these messages and inviting them to have their say, which is how we truly get to know ourselves in an accepting, compassionate way.

In many ways, compassion unlocks it all. Compassion is at the heart of community and humanity as well as our work against trauma. And when it comes to post-trauma growth and resilience, compassion rules.

It's not true that what doesn't kill us makes us stronger. What doesn't kill us can actually leave us with wounds that make life a lot more difficult. That being said, what doesn't kill us can make us wiser, more grateful, and more compassionate. And when it comes to the bigger picture—not only helping ourselves but also helping others and the world—compassion makes all the difference.

The Murder That Wasn't and the Assault That Was

I once took care of a man who had lived a violent life, with long prison sentences and a history of thumbing his nose at societal norms. He was a self-identified hardened criminal who came to see me later in his life because he was trying to be a better person. He'd recently become a grandparent, and this was the primary incentive to change his life. The man did excellent work in therapy, and he never missed appointments.

Months into our work together, another man committed a terrible crime against someone in my patient's family. My patient broke into the man's home and waited for him to return so that he could kill him for what he had done. While waiting, he started reflecting on what he was about to do, thinking about what it would mean to the other person's family and to his own grandchild as well. After a while of allowing himself both to think and feel through what he was doing and how he felt about it, my patient decided to leave. He snuck out of the house and went home.

As he told me the story, he almost couldn't believe it. He had actually chosen not to be violent. He'd recognized that the revenge he had in mind wouldn't bring justice and that the cascade of consequences following such a violent act certainly wasn't worth it. He told me all of this with bashful pride.

That's a success story in itself, but that's not all.

A few months later, a young patient came to my office early in the morning after having been assaulted the previous night. I had walk-in hours scheduled for mid-morning, and she came to use one of those last-minute spots. A receptionist rushed in to tell me that the young woman was sitting in the waiting room—wearing torn clothing, bleeding from cuts and scrapes, and crying quietly. I ran out to the waiting room to see her, and there she was, sitting across from the so-called hardened criminal, my next scheduled appointment. He'd been in the waiting room when she had arrived.

This man—who'd spent so much time in prison and so much of his life breaking the rules and being violent—was a real help to the woman, and he did everything right. He kept his distance so that she'd feel safe, but he also reassured her that she was about to get help, that she was safe and okay. I watched all of this from the doorway. He let the young woman take his appointment and stayed in the waiting room until the first walk-in spot opened.

I'm happy to say that the young woman received helpful treatment and went on to make some healthy life changes as a result of what happened to her. I'm also happy to say that the exchange between her and the "hardened criminal" had a profound impact on his life.

He felt himself softening. He was also proud of how helpful he'd been to the woman ("just like a normal person would do," he said) and how effortlessly he'd reached out to her. And he was also quite aware that he wouldn't have been in the waiting room to help her had he killed the man a few months back. Even if he'd gotten away with it, would he have had the humanity to reach out the way he did?

This is a man with a trauma history a mile long, both suffering from trauma and inflicting it upon others. But when it came time to choose which way to keep going in his life, he chose compassion. He'd become aware that trauma begets more trauma. Finally understanding that is what helped him to reroute his life.

REFLECTION This story is about a lot of things, including help from an unlikely source and the ways we can surprise ourselves unexpectedly for the better. Think about your own life and a time when you chose the healthier, less trauma-inflicting option at a crossroads. Would you have made the same choice at a different stage of life? What helped steer you in the right direction? What elements of compassion, community, and humanity can you find in the choice you made?

CHAPTER 14

Leading with Wisdom, Patience, and a True Life Narrative

Covid-19, forest fires, systemic racism, politically motivated threats and violence, income disparity, the loss of employment and health benefits . . . the societal traumas facing us today call out for us to help one another and finally recognize the fact of our global interconnectedness. You can accept and embrace who you are right now. You can accept and embrace gaining the knowledge you need in order to change and changing in order to gain more knowledge. And you can also start by *doing*—by making someone's life a little better today, by making a difference locally, by advocating for a global cause. Your entry points for positive action are literally endless. The difference any of one of us can make individually is impossible to gauge, and that's all the more reason for us to work together.

LEADING WITH WISDOM AND PATIENCE

Facing our own trauma and doing our part in the larger healing doesn't mean we have to become scholars or saints. What I'm suggesting here isn't that lofty, and it certainly isn't abstract. Wisdom and patience come with compassionate, common-sense changes in our lives; straightforward solutions that don't exactly come easily. Wisdom and patience aren't qualities we either have or don't have; they are embodied attributes that grow stronger with practice.

Wisdom and patience arise when we experience ourselves and others through the lens of compassion, when we see through the lies trauma wants us to believe about ourselves, and when we see how trauma influences our affects, feelings, and emotions. Wisdom and patience also occur every time we feel something powerful and intense arise in us, and we choose to wait and reflect instead of instantly reacting. Wisdom and patience come from putting words to all of the thoughts and messages arising in us and from sharing our needs and wants with others. And we foster our growing wisdom and patience every time we make an intentional decision and see the degree to which trauma has previously made our decisions for us.

With wisdom and patience, we become our best self. Again, the goal isn't perfection. In fact, a need for perfection is one of the lies trauma tries to get us to believe. The goal isn't a constantly moving goalpost, but a heartfelt pledge to keep our best interests in mind as well as the best interests of others. The goal is to become self-led and, in the process, lead others to become so as well.

Wise and patient judgments help us to lead and also help us to know when to be led. We're surrounded by leaders in our families, neighborhoods, cities, and countries. Telling helpful leaders apart from those committed only to their own self-interest is crucial, and it requires relying on time-tested values such as compassion, community, and humanity. Are our leaders truly committed to these? Are we?

Trauma scrambles the picture, but we're all capable of determining these answers and becoming good judges of ourselves and others. As a physician and practicing psychiatrist, I'm struck by how often brain biology and psychology align to teach us the same lesson—that we're all creatures of habit, for example. We see this blatantly not only on the physiological level but also in the realm of human behaviors. Changing what's ingrained in us—especially when it comes to trauma—requires practice, perseverance, and compassion. It also takes wisdom and patience, and we need all of these qualities to become good judges and effective leaders.

We all have it in ourselves to lead in some way. After we have the requisite knowledge and support, it's up to us to decide whether trauma is going to lead us or we're going to lead in the face of trauma. We can put a stop to the horrible cycles of shame and risk; we don't have to leave the legacy of trauma for future generations. We can choose to lead, to define healthier paths forward, and to create a better world for all of us.

CLEAR COMMUNICATION

In building a world that handles existing trauma better, we also need to ensure we're doing everything we can to avoid various mechanisms that empower or create more trauma. This is no more obvious than in the sphere of communication. In a world seduced by fake news outlets, the spread of Internet rumors and lies, and public leaders who flout the truth in bombastic and binary ways, we all could do a better job at paying attention to the language we use. Language is crucial in conveying our beliefs and feelings—especially in our mutual work against trauma—but we also must remember that language evokes particular beliefs and feelings in others. Accordingly, we need to wield language more carefully, and we should expect our leaders to do the same.

The use of strong negative language in public venues has become much more prevalent in recent years. This includes the insults and threats that permeate some aspects of social media and cable news—ways of speaking and writing that would have commanded widespread disapproval in the past. How we express ourselves and speak to others has a profound impact on the type of world we're creating. Disdainful labels and exaggerated speech alienate and disempower people, and the most vulnerable among us are typically the most affected by weaponized language. With that said, as leaders and citizens committed to stopping the spread of trauma, here are four practical ways to communicate more clearly and more authentically:

1 **AVOID EXAGGERATIONS.** A flood that devastates a town is *horrible* and *terrible*. Using words like *horrible* and *terrible* to describe the results of a democratic election you don't like or people who have different political opinions than you cheapens the descriptive power such words hold and diminishes their true meaning.

2 **ABSTAIN FROM LABELING.** Far too often, language is employed to generate false similarities and false differences between groups of people. This applies to the two political colors we affiliate with states, to gender and sexuality, to race, and to the nature of our origin in our given country. For example, the word *immigrant* is used as a charged and binary term in the United States despite the fact that most of the people in the country are here today as a result of immigration.

3 **DON'T TRIVIALIZE.** Qualifiers that trivialize especially matter when the topic under consideration involves personal trauma and doubly so when the topic is about a type of widespread societal trauma. For example, I'm regularly alarmed at how the term "sexual assault" is employed in health care and the media to minimize the severity of the violence endured, as if the assault were somehow excusable or less impactful because of the sexual nature of the attack. Trivializing traumatic experiences in an offhanded way might not be deliberate, but it can create more trauma nonetheless.

4 **THINK ABOUT THE IMPACT.** This suggestion applies to the examples above and to countless others. One example that deeply troubles me is the use of the term "burned out" to describe what happens to people in the health-care industry after they've reached their breaking point in a system that overworks and devalues them. Instead of decrying problems in the system, the impact of such a term places the responsibility on individual people, unfairly implying weakness and lack of self-care. When we don't think about the language we use to describe others, we can often become accomplices to trauma, fueling shame in others as opposed to working with them to right unhealthy environments.

Exercising kindness, clarity, and mindfulness in our communication isn't all it will take to halt trauma, but it's a good place to start. And those of us who choose to lead in some capacity owe it to ourselves and those who look to us for guidance to do a much better job at it.

Do You Know What That Word Means?

Medical students accomplish part of their education during clinical rotations, which usually occur in hospitals. In a clinical rotation, a student follows a team of doctors for a certain number of weeks, and the purpose of doing so is to learn by observing, researching, and participating in patient care.

Sometimes a student is integrated into the team and has a good sense of what's being done. Other times, especially when the team is large and includes doctors of varying levels of seniority, a student can get lost in the shuffle. While assigned to this kind of clinical rotation, I learned an important lesson about authority, fear, and how words can be traumatizing to others, even on accident.

When I followed the team through the hospital corridors, I felt like a particle of dust at the end of a comet. The senior doctor was at the front, with other doctors following behind in order of seniority, usually in groups of two or three. The other students and I trailed behind them, our presence usually an afterthought to the main body of this medical comet. We didn't have much authority, but we were certainly in a different position than the people who were sick. I'm thinking now of one patient in particular—an elderly man I'd met only once before.

The man seemed frightened to be in the hospital and away from home. His anxiety ratcheted up even more when all of us—a roving crowd of white coats and serious faces—abruptly filed into his room. I was closest to the door (which happens when you're at the back of the comet), but I was also tall enough to see over the shoulders of the other students and doctors. Because this visit was all very routine for the team, everyone seemed focused on considerations other than the patient—the next patient in line, documenting the visit, an upcoming research paper, and so on. Whatever it was, nobody was paying much attention to the patient himself.

The senior doctor summarized the man's test results and explained the diagnosis: cancer. The doctor went on to explain the type of cancer but not the fact that this version was curable in nearly all cases. The elderly man just stared ahead and listened. Then the senior doctor said, with an air of professional distance, that an oncologist would come by later in the day. At this point, the patient's eyes widened, and the color drained from his face. He looked as if he'd seen a ghost.

After we completed our rounds on the floor, I kept thinking about that look. Something about the patient's reaction felt off to me, so I slipped away and returned to check in on him. He still looked shocked and afraid, but he was friendly and seemed open to my visit.

"You seemed really upset about the oncologist," I said.

He nodded and swallowed hard.

"Sir, do you know what the word *oncologist* means?" I asked.

"I think so," he said. "It means an undertaker, right?"

I explained the difference between the two occupations and made sure the patient knew that his cancer was treatable and that the oncologist would explain the course of treatment later. The relief on his face was incredible. He apologized for his confusion, but I told him that the team owed him an apology.

This is just one example of how we can use words to serve ourselves instead of the people we're supposed to be communicating with. If the lead doctor had been paying more attention, maybe the patient would have been spared all of that unnecessary distress. The key to communicating isn't just in speaking the most accurate words but in noting how those words affect others, listening better, and attending to their body language in a more skillful way. If we did so, our communication would be more effective, and we would also trigger others less and be less apt to create new trauma. Considering what words mean to us as well as what they mean to others—and paying attention to how our communication is being received by them—is crucial. This is important when it comes to conveying information and even more so when it comes to racially or sexually charged topics and words.

REFLECTION What are some words you have used with others—recently or in the more distant past—that had a triggering effect without you intending such? How did you know that your language bothered the person?

How did you receive that message? What changes did you make in the ways you communicate with that feedback in mind? What words bother you that are seemingly innocuous to others?

THE IMPORTANCE OF STORIES AND A TRUE LIFE NARRATIVE

Words create sentences, sentences create stories, and stories are our way of understanding our lives and the world. Stories help us understand the lessons we've learned, helpful and unhelpful, and it's often beneficial to revisit our stories, especially the ones that affect us in negative ways. Our brains don't naturally like to reassess the truth claims of the lessons we've experienced—in other words, we don't go back and question if the lessons are telling us the truth. We simply craft a story about their meaning, accept them, and move on. And when these lessons are trauma-related, we often get saddled with negative consequences without being aware of it, maybe because trauma lessons tend to be "stickier"—that is, they're strongly attached to negative affects, feelings, and emotions.

I can think of a few examples from my own life: I always received good grades in school, so I accept that I'm intelligent. I've done reasonably well in my career, so I accept that I'm able to buckle down and work hard. These are positive aspects of my personal story, but they're mundane to me—I don't reflect on them, celebrate them, or think about them much at all. Any negative aspects, however, are a different story entirely. Even a moderately true and mildly negative thing I think about myself can take up an extraordinary amount of space in my brain—for example, I'm not that good at throwing a ball. I can toss a baseball around fairly well (it took a lot of practice), but when it comes to a football, forget it. So, when I was growing up, I made some conclusions about myself being uncoordinated and therefore destined for mockery and athletic failure.

As life progressed and tragedies became part of my experience, it became easier for me to pick up the story that I was a failure and therefore marked for unhappiness. Like some people, I often felt I was cursed, a difficult thing to believe about oneself and a disputable life lesson that can affect mood, anxiety levels, and decision making. At some point, this negative story about myself took root, but I never stopped to challenge it at the time. That's what we need to do if we want to see ourselves clearly and break free from the damaging stories trauma would like us to believe.

Trauma paints over our varied experiences with an awkwardly broad brush, covering the good lessons and then scrawling frightening script over them that tells us hurtful things about ourselves: "Nothing good ever happens to me," "Everyone is out to get me," or "No one will ever love me," for example. Trauma clouds our achievements and robs us of the joy and satisfaction that are rightfully ours: instead of "I faced that difficult task and earned success," we get "I got lucky, but it probably won't happen again" or "Yeah, I won that time, but it doesn't matter, because I don't deserve to win because I'm _____" (whatever fits best at the time: miserable, unlovable, bad, and so on).

Damaging stories about ourselves are sort of like myths that no one really wants to read but that get knitted together anyway into the collection of stories that become our false life narrative. A false life narrative amplifies negative stories, forgets or hides positive ones, stifles any present evidence that might challenge our views about ourselves, and projects the promise of repetitive negativity into the future. Trauma is the author of these false narratives, and if we don't take an active hand in the editing process, we'll be stuck with stories that work against us.

In fact, we can take the pen away from trauma altogether and write our own *true life narratives*. These narratives treat us with respect and fairness. They acknowledge our courage and the effort it takes to make even the smallest triumph happen. A true life narrative recognizes what it takes to raise children, support a family, proclaim one's gender identity, embrace one's sexuality, persevere despite racism, or continue one's degree after an assault. True life narratives are honest, inspiring, and serve us in the face of trauma. They're also the blueprints of our future.

ANTIDOTE: *Writing Your True Life Narrative*

It's important to revisit, question, and rewrite the hurtful stories we carry with us. It's equally or more important to replace those stories with a narrative that actually benefits us. A true life narrative is something we can do on our own through reflection and writing, but it can be truly beneficial to have someone we trust help us with the process—a good friend, for example, or a therapist. No matter how we create our true life narrative, it's crucial that we see ourselves with clarity and compassion.

Creating a true life narrative is like waking up in the backseat of a car being driven by a reckless phantom. We climb over the seat, shove the phantom aside, and take the wheel. After we're in the driver's seat, it's not so hard to check the mirrors, adjust the seat, and decide where we'd like to go in life. No more phantom zooming around, cussing at us and telling us hurtful stories. The phantom was only in charge as long as we were asleep in the backseat; after we banish it, it's gone. As an added bonus, being better drivers means that we make the road safer for others as well.

The Girl Whose Name Was Changed

I knew a young woman who grew up in a war-torn country in which the level of violence defies imagination. Her earliest memories were of fear and loss. When she was a child, the surviving members of her family fled to a remote jungle. Although they were safer from violence in the jungle, the living conditions were nearly impossible, and she and the people with her rarely had enough food. They suffered from rampant disease.

Despite these challenges, the girl was loved and nurtured. She remembers being held by her mother and father and being reassured that she was wonderful and important. Most of all, she remembers being loved. As she grew into her teens, she proved to be quick-witted, savvy, selfless, and brave. There came a crucial time in which her people's camp had to move because the bog they were using to grow food had become clogged and a flood was likely to destroy their camp.

She remembers how the men looked when they came back from unsuccessfully trying to free the clog and thereby fix the problem. They looked afraid but were also calm because of the impossibility of the situation. She also clearly remembers the difference between her and the men—she was small and lithe, whereas they were fully grown. Thinking about that difference, she decided that she would fix the problem. She waded into the bog, swam through the water teeming with snakes and parasites, and struggled to the back of the bog. She was able to pull out the giant leaves and other debris that had clogged the outlet. It worked, and the water began to flow smoothly again.

This girl was given a particular name at birth, and she liked it very much, but she didn't use it anymore. After she saved the camp, her family and the rest of her people held a ceremony and gave her a new name to recognize her heroism, reflect her character, and announce her as a person of grace and strength.

Despite growing up in truly horrible circumstances, this young woman always knew she mattered. She knew who she was and had confidence in herself, and when the time came, she simply did what had to be done. Later in her life, she went on to thrive with new opportunities, earned a good education, and took valuable skills back to her community to help them. Loving and nurturing a child—even under the worst of circumstances—can bring out the best in them, especially when it most matters. One version of this story says that her parents had little to give her; a better version acknowledges that they gave her everything.

REFLECTION Think of a time when you triumphed despite the odds being stacked against you. What qualities in yourself did you call upon to succeed? Who helped you along the way? What role could this accomplishment play in your own true life narrative? What can it tell you about yourself in the face of future trials?

CHAPTER 15

A Humanist Social Commitment

My goal for the end of this book is to send you off with new motivation and multiple tools and ideas to counter trauma and the damage it does to us. To that end, I'd like to present my case for a humanist social commitment and invite you to join me.

As I've stated elsewhere in this book, trauma isn't just an individual issue, and our own personal solutions are unlikely to change the big picture enough to make a lasting difference. That said, all of our efforts together can create the substantive change I believe most of us crave and need. Together, we can banish trauma from our bodies and homes, from our loved ones and communities, and from our nation and planet. Together, we can prevent trauma from taking root, and we can create an environment devoted to true healing. But all of this won't just happen on its own; we must work for it, and we must work together.

OUR COMMITMENT

I believe most of us are already familiar with the foundations and goals of a humanist social commitment. We know them from the compassionate teachings of the world's religions, and they were presented to us as the democratic ideals upon which our country is founded. We're faced with significant challenges today, and it can feel as if our shared traumas are spinning out of control, but I firmly believe we can rely on these foundations and goals to see us through.

First and foremost, a humanist social commitment embraces respect for all people—including ourselves and those quite different from us. Part of placing such a high value on respect is accepting that we are fallible and understanding that our beliefs and feelings don't necessarily encompass all truths. Accordingly, unless we're speaking about basic math or agreed-upon phenomena such as gravity, a humanist social commitment means exercising care in deciding what's true and making claims regarding that truth. We must understand that we can sometimes be misled and that trauma is often the misleader.

Being aligned with a humanist social commitment means remembering that the wide variety of human beliefs and feelings are based on infinitely complex factors ranging from trauma exposure, genetics, culture of origin, family dynamics, privilege, and disfranchisement to stage of life and so on. We can believe in something quite strongly while at the same time allowing for others to hold different beliefs. This takes humility and compassion, and it promotes an environment of acceptance, trust, and mutual safety.

FIVE FOUNDATIONS

Human societies are shaped by the values they instill in their people as well as how the people come to embody those values through their own experience, education, and actions. These are the components that enliven and describe any society, and I propose we incorporate the following five foundations when establishing a humanist social commitment.

1 **HISTORY.** History helps us understand how we got to where we are as a society and collection of societies. A circumspect reading of history informs us of our shared and diverse origins, the consequences of war and greed, and the benefits and detriments of progress. History clarifies political events and gives us a comparative foundation with which to place ourselves in time.

2 **RELIGION.** I'm not referring to religion for religion's sake but instead to the shared values at the heart of most of the world's religious traditions, especially those values embracing compassion and respect for life. Along with science, religion

grounds our understanding of our place in the universe, and it's also at the core of our sense of life meaning and purpose.

3 **SCIENCE AND MEDICINE.** Science and medicine teach us how the universe works and how our brains and bodies exist within it. They make sense of the microscopic and the cosmic and everything in between. They also ground our understanding of cause and effect and describe what social transformation can look like.

4 **LIFE EXPERIENCE.** We filter everything through our life experience. All the other four points on this list of foundations are funneled through our own perceptions, filters, and relationships. Life experience is learning embodied—the combination of our limbic systems and logic systems affecting our convictions and intentions.

5 **EARLY EDUCATION.** The basics of education—such as those we learn in kindergarten—are rooted in kindness, humility, and common sense. Although we often forget these lessons later in life, early education teaches us that the secrets of understanding and happiness are actually quite simple.

We can rely on one or more of these foundations for nearly everything in life. For example, when it comes to trauma, history clearly illustrates the damages of large-scale violence, religion stresses the value of treating others with kindness and taking care of those in need, science and medicine outline how to prevent and treat trauma, life experience empowers us to call upon our own sorrows and joys to relate to others, and early education instills in us straightforward teachings to promote compassion, community, and humanity.

THE BIOPSYCHOSOCIAL-SPIRITUAL MODEL

The biopsychosocial model was developed by an American physician, George Engel, in the 1970s as a way to comprehensively understand human health. It has become a primary approach to mental health care over the years and has expanded to include spiritual and cultural elements (accordingly, it's often now called the *biopsychosocial-spiritual model*). In its own way, this model is an approach to health care that takes the five foundations listed above to heart. When used fully, this model captures limitless ways of helping and healing. It considers genetics, the various influences that determine how our genes function, brain biology, psychotherapeutic treatments, Western and indigenous medicines, nutrition, cultural background, social circles, personality, personal histories, education, religious and spiritual values, and so on. This model also places a premium on what's called agency—the ability to understand and navigate the world in the ways we choose. This doesn't mean the ways chosen by the loudest and most fearful (i.e., traumatized) parts of us but instead the ways chosen by our whole selves. The spiritual aspect of the biopsychosocial-spiritual model can be considered the force that binds together all of these parts into a living whole—a human actively being in the world. Spirituality can be expressed through religion or outside of traditional religions, but ideally it embraces compassion and tolerance. Spirituality allows us to feel responsibility to people beyond ourselves and our loved ones, and it also instills the desire to promote justice for all people. If we strive to be our best selves from all of these angles—biological, psychological, social, and spiritual—our brains, bodies, and spirits will serve us as best they can. This is especially true when it comes to trauma—understanding it, preventing it, and treating it—for ourselves, other people, and the world.

FIVE GOALS

Our humanist social commitment is grounded in the five foundations listed above, but it takes more than ground to get things done. Here are the five action-oriented goals I believe we must dedicate ourselves to in order to triumph over trauma and create a truly democratic, just society free of human-caused trauma:

1 **CONSIDER OURSELVES AND OTHERS WITH COMPASSION.** So much of our lives are lived inside of our heads, and what we think

and tell ourselves there matters immensely. This is where we can harbor angry or hopeless thoughts, which can then turn into destructive fantasies, which can eventually turn into destructive realities. Our minds are the places where we can berate ourselves repeatedly, beating ourselves down without the need for any outside persecutor to do it for us. So, the first goal begins with us transforming whatever trauma might be occurring inside of us and replacing what's toxic with compassionate thinking. First, we need to be aware of our own thought patterns, and I've briefly offered some proven techniques to help with that. We can also use our own understanding and other innovations offered by science (e.g., psychotherapy and psychiatry) and religious traditions (e.g., mindfulness and prayer) to foster a mental environment marked by kindness and compassion.

2 **ACT WITHOUT HARMING OURSELVES OR OTHERS.** The ancient Greek physician Hippocrates (considered the Western "father of medicine") asked physicians to first commit to do no harm. *Ahimsa*—"nonviolence"—is a primary principle in Buddhism, Hinduism, and Jainism. Not making things worse is the first step in making things better, and we must commit to the former for the latter to truly take root. Not doing so is the same as putting the cart before the proverbial horse. This goal itself requires a fundamental commitment to the first goal because compassion empowers our resolve not to be pulled around by blind, self-serving impulses without a thought about the consequences. Doing no harm isn't an absence of activity; it actually takes conscious effort, especially when trauma has hijacked our limbic system.

3 **TREAT OURSELVES AND OTHERS WITH COMPASSION.** When Mahatma Gandhi advised us to become the change we want to see in the world, he wasn't advocating for some magical caterpillar-to-butterfly transformation. Instead, Gandhi was guiding us to work hard to have more say in what goes on both inside and outside of us. On the surface, this goal might seem the same as the first, but treating ourselves and others with compassion involves more than thought—it takes action and presence in

the world. And it's more than refraining from generating more trauma; it's about employing our compassion in practical ways to decrease the power and impact of trauma in the world.

4 **LEARN AND EDUCATE.** We must commit ourselves to lifelong learning and also to teaching others, especially the children entrusted to our care. Ideally, this book has been educational, but it certainly isn't the last word on trauma. We need to constantly examine our stories and thought patterns and guide ourselves with clarity and compassion. We also need to instill in our children an education that empowers their resilience to trauma. Education also means learning to see through the contrived and self-serving agendas advanced by others (often through ever-present media), especially when they involve attempts to justify trauma-inducing practices through religious, political, social, or legal arguments.

5 **DEMAND ACCOUNTABILITY.** Accountability is the mechanism that ensures our commitment to the previous goals. It's also our way to state clear expectations of others, especially those in positions of power—political and otherwise. The more we hold ourselves and others accountable to compassion in thought and deed, nonviolence, and the knowledge that comes from education, the more effective we'll be in our efforts against trauma. It's also how we can work together to build a world that reflects upon us better as a species.

Ten Years Later, Ten Years Younger

Ten years ago, I met a woman who came to my office to treat her depression. She was only middle aged, but she appeared much older. This patient was obviously fatigued, and it was clear she wasn't taking good care of herself. While taking her history, I learned of the tragic loss that had struck her several years prior, but she relayed the story of it factually and almost incidentally, as if it had little to do with the state she was in now.

She was surprised when I talked about trauma and the impact I believed it was having upon her. She strongly stated that the tragedy was in the past, but her depression was occurring quite clearly in the present—her terrible insomnia, for example, or her new beliefs that life was hopeless and that she couldn't accomplish anything good no matter how hard she might try. However, she was willing to consider that trauma might be playing a role, at least when it came to her anxiety. She decided to accept treatment, which consisted of therapy and two medicines—one medicine to improve her mood and her tolerance of distress and the other to help her sleep.

She responded remarkably well to the therapy and the medicines. She was able to return to work, learned some new skills, and began offering her time and energy by volunteering to help people in need. She also committed herself to a healthier diet, exercise, social life, and some exploration and excitement. The treatment worked so well that I don't get the pleasure of her company much anymore. What most amazes me on the rare occasion I do get to see her is how much younger she looks—it's been an entire decade since we first met, and yet she looks strikingly younger than she did so many years ago! The person she lost—the one connected to her profound disheartenment and resultant depression—would undoubtedly be proud of her. I've never known anyone to recover better from trauma.

REFLECTION This story seems like a straightforward tale of success, but the truth is that this woman fully committed herself to facing her trauma and doing what it took to come out on the other side. In one way or the other, she manifested each of the five goals listed above in order to fully recover and thrive. For this final reflection, I want to invite you to think about what your own success story might look like and contemplate how the five goals offered here will help you make that story a reality. What would thinking with more compassion look like for you? What harm(s) could you stop committing against yourself or others? Think of two or three tangible acts of compassion you could make. What do you need to learn in order to help yourself and others, and what do you have to teach? Finally, and with compassion, how can you better hold yourself and others accountable?

CLOSING THOUGHTS

As I write this, I realize it's been more than twenty-five years since Jonathan's death. I think about how I've moved forward with my life, how the milestones I've achieved along the way speak to striving and perseverance. I can honor all of that and at the same time acknowledge that the shock and aftermath of my brother's suicide still affect me today. It goes without saying that I'm not the same person I was before he died, and part of that comes out in a prevailing sense of vulnerability and anxiety that gets worse whenever a new trauma strikes and tries to convince me that my self-care will never be enough. On the other hand, when I feel supported, when positive things happen, and when I take good care of myself, I get a sense of what's meant by the word *thriving*. Then I feel bolstered by gratitude for the people who love me, and I feel happy and full of purpose. My brother's suicide will always hurt, but it's also brought me some hard-earned wisdom I'll share with you now to close out the book:

- First, healing from trauma often takes heartfelt grieving, but trauma gets in grieving's way with anger, guilt, shame, and blame.

- Because trauma burdens us, disorients us, and disheartens us, we need help that only other people can provide.

- We need to accept that help. We also need to give it.

- Sometimes the only help we can give or receive is the willingness to sit with what feels unbearable. If we can do that, trauma inevitably loosens its grip over time—enough, at least, to allow the light to shine in and healing to begin.

- Finally, trauma isn't just an individual issue. An indispensable part of helping is standing against ignorance, prejudice, and malice and standing *for* compassion, community, and humanity.

At the beginning of this book, I said that my purpose was to sound the alarm about trauma. I hope I've done that. I've tried my best to describe what trauma is and what it does to us and also give you some analogies and stories from real life to illustrate how trauma works. Trauma affects all of us—individuals, families, communities, and nations—and its consequences are dramatic and real. I find it hard to imagine an enemy more dangerous than one that's so damaging while also being so hard to see. Trauma makes us conflicted about who we are, what we deserve, and what we're capable of achieving. By altering our brains, trauma changes the filters we use to perceive the world and makes it difficult to see ourselves and others with clarity. For all of these reasons and more, we must bring trauma to light. We can't allow it to be invisible any longer.

When we understand trauma better and get it out in front of us, we can call upon our knowledge, compassion, and resolve to do something about it. Whether through the five goals offered in this chapter, the various self-care antidotes mentioned elsewhere, or the assistance of others, we can move forward through trauma to thrive and improve the world we inhabit. But we have to start by opening our eyes to the severity of the problem.

For most people—myself included—there was a time before trauma and a time after. Sometimes it can feel impossible to access the person you once were, and trauma in early childhood can make it quite difficult to connect to any sense of fundamental safety and goodness. Childhood trauma often leads to self-blame because a child's mind has yet to develop enough to place responsibility where it belongs—on the perpetrator of violence, for example. In these cases, we're typically left feeling like there's something basically wrong with us as opposed to other people being the issue. Our brains don't typically challenge our messages of self-blame and shame, so it's all the more important as adults to find ways to reroute those thoughts into positive, life-affirming messages that are both clear and compassionate. The truth is out there; it's just that we're often facing in the wrong direction to see it.

Before trauma scrawled all over the maps we were born with, they showed us where we were and how to get around. On a map untouched by trauma, we can draw paths almost anywhere we wish to go, explore life's terrain, navigate the struggles and challenges of life, and eventually find our way home. We want that map back—not just for ourselves but for others, too. We want reliable signposts that don't lead any of us astray. We want to be able to travel life from coast to coast, discover the goodness that's our birthright, form valuable memories, join other travelers along the way, and lend a helping hand where it's needed.

In the introduction, I wrote, "The diversity of human problems I have witnessed in my life and career is nearly infinite. That being said, one reason stands out for the vast majority of these problems—the underlying reason is trauma." I still think this is an incredibly hopeful statement because having one reason to address makes our task obvious and straightforward. We must address trauma. We don't have to believe its lies any longer. We're not doomed to suffering more trauma or to creating more trauma for others. In fact, quite the opposite is true. With compassion, community, and humanity, we have all the power we need. Power enough to deal with trauma. Power enough to change.

Acknowledgments

I am thankful for the good people who have helped me to learn, persevere, contribute back to the world, and find expanded horizons along the way. I am grateful for the hands that have guided me to and from youth and the responsibilities and joys of adulthood. My parents, Richard and Theresa Conti, gave me all the good things parents can give, and my mother is deeply missed since her passing in 2011. I am thankful for my brother Thomas and his family and for the time I had with my brother Jonathan.

My wife, Dr. Brooke Maylie, has taught me a great deal about coping with trauma with grace and resolve, and I feel immense gratitude for every discovery and every smile of our two children, Colette and Amelie. This feeling extends to Jovita Parnell and her family and to Brooke's family for their support over the years.

My maternal grandmother, Grace Venanzi, was the ultimate nurturing presence in my life, and I am thankful for her extended family, including my Aunt Rose and Uncle Rango. My paternal grandparents modeled fortitude and ambition, and I am thankful for their extended family, including Julie and Rob; Maureen, Joe, Jessica, and Julia; Christine and Bryan; Ryan, who served our country with honor; and my Aunt Barbara Kellam Ollarvia, who blazed the family path to authorship!

Mary Ann Frascella and Steve Materia have given special gifts to my family, and Brittany Jo Nieman imparted gifts to me that have only grown since her untimely passing.

I am thankful for Sandy Zarodnansky and for all those who taught me over the years. This includes mentors and colleagues at Stanford and Harvard, with particular thanks to Dr. Mary Anne Badaracco, Dr. Jose and Sandra

Delgado, and Dr. Justin Birnbaum. The therapeutic guidance and wisdom of Dr. N. Gregory Hamilton have helped me to navigate my life, and Dr. Rita Swan and Dr. Seth Asser set examples for commitment to others. I am also thankful for Stephanie zu Guttenberg and Dr. Daryn Reicherter, who took the time to have conversations that immeasurably improve this book.

And where would I be without the people I have been honored to care for? I could write an endless list, with special thanks to Stefani Germanotta for her trust in me, her kind encouragement, and her generous contribution to this book. I have special thanks for Amanda and Wendy and for the memory of John, his art, and his many fish.

I am blessed with wonderfully supportive friends who have enriched my life beyond measure. I am fortunate to have a very long list, with special gratitude to Joe Vasta, Mr. and Mrs. Vasta, and Jason Pyle; Nancy Brunner; Dave and Pantea Hannauer and their families; Mike Martin; Peter and Jill Attia; Bobby Dery; Zol Kryger; Matt McCormack; Joanna Staunton; Frank Crivelli; Rob McDonald; Bob Skillman; Chris Ducko; Josh Smith; Mihir Goswami and Peder Anderlind; and the memory of Michael Dass.

Without Amber Blum I would be, to put it simply, lost, and she and Carmen Hepner Hall have been outstanding colleagues and friends, as has Dr. Andy Mendenhall, a dedicated and compassionate practice partner. I thank all of the good people I have worked with, especially my compatriots at Pacific Premier Group, PC. Dr. Jim Kochalka has become a friend and mentor, and the support of Dr. Bernard Kruger, and of Patrick Bryson and Peter Schalk, has been invaluable to me.

I am grateful to Tommy Hilfiger for helping me decide to write this book and to Tim Ferriss for his friendship and his guidance as I sorted through initial concepts. I have the highest praise for Robert Lee, the editor who took on a first-time author and dedicated tremendous effort and acumen to making this the best book it can be. The whole project was guided forward by Jaime Schwalb, and I am thankful for the confidence she and others at Sounds True have had in me.

Bibliography

Gilbert, Olive. *Narrative of Sojourner Truth*. New York: Penguin, 1998.

Mansfield, Katherine. "Her First Ball." In *The Garden Party and Other Stories*. New York: Knopf, 1922.

Rilke, Rainer Maria. "Buddha in Glory." In *Ahead of All Parting: The Selected Poetry and Prose of Rainer Maria Rilke*, translated by Stephen Mitchell. New York: Random House, 1995.

Wiesel, Elie. *Night*. Translated by Stella Rodway. New York: Bantam, 1982.

About the Author

Paul Conti was born and raised in Trenton, New Jersey. He was educated at public schools in Hamilton, a suburb of Trenton. His mother was a teacher, and his father founded a real estate company. Paul attended college at the University of Pennsylvania, also studying abroad in England, and he graduated summa cum laude in political science and mathematics. A four-year career in consulting followed, with four months of travel in the middle. With no science coursework and a wish to go to medical school, Paul attended the intensive premed program at Bryn Mawr College and was subsequently admitted to Stanford Medical School. He spent seven years there, including psychiatry training, with internal medicine and neurology rotations. Paul eventually became a chief resident at Harvard, where he won a teaching award and remained on the faculty. After moving to Portland, Paul was named one of Oregon's Top Physicians in his first year of practice. His current work includes diagnostic evaluation and treatment with psychotherapy and medication. Paul also provides neurobiological education as well as business, legal, and personal health optimization consulting. He has founded two clinics over the past decade, with his current work through Pacific Premier Group, PC. This clinic provides a setting for like-minded people to practice and consult together, sharing expertise and a drive for excellence. Paul has offices in Portland and New York and works with patients and clients across the United States and abroad. His interests are diverse, mostly revolving around human beings and their subjective experience of life. He is grateful for his many blessings, including his brave and widely accomplished wife, his two insightful and irrepressible daughters, and the family and friends who have guided him forward when he has found himself adrift.

About Sounds True

Sounds True is a multimedia publisher whose mission is to inspire and support personal transformation and spiritual awakening. Founded in 1985 and located in Boulder, Colorado, we work with many of the leading spiritual teachers, thinkers, healers, and visionary artists of our time. We strive with every title to preserve the essential "living wisdom" of the author or artist. It is our goal to create products that not only provide information to a reader or listener but also embody the quality of a wisdom transmission.

For those seeking genuine transformation, Sounds True is your trusted partner. At SoundsTrue.com you will find a wealth of free resources to support your journey, including exclusive weekly audio interviews, free downloads, interactive learning tools, and other special savings on all our titles.

To learn more, please visit SoundsTrue.com/freegifts or call us toll-free at 800.333.9185.